eliminating world poverty

making governance work for the poor

A White Paper on International Development

Presented to Parliament
by the Secretary of State for International Development
by Command of Her Majesty

July 2006

Cm 6876 | £24

contents

Foreword by the Prime Minister ii

Preface: the challenge for our generation iii
This White Paper xi

Delivering our promises

Chapter 1 Delivering the promises of 2005 2
The case for development 3
Poverty is falling, but progress is uneven 6
Making progress against the 2005 commitments 9

Building states that work for poor people

Chapter 2 Building effective states and better governance ... 18
Good governance is essential to reduce poverty 19
Improving governance 21
The UK will use its aid to support good governance 23
International partners can help 25
Winning the fight against corruption 28

Chapter 3 Supporting good governance internationally ... 32
Governance is an international issue 33
International standards encourage responsible behaviour .. 34
International standards help fight corruption 37
International standards promote better governance 40

Helping people get security, incomes, and public services

Chapter 4 Promoting peace and security 44
Insecurity and conflict keep people poor 45
Improving security and preventing conflict 46
Tackling conflict and building peace 49

Chapter 5 Reducing poverty through economic growth ... 56
Growth is the best way to reduce poverty 57
Promoting growth 58
Helping poor people to benefit from growth 64
Using natural resources for sustainable growth 66
Opening up trade 67
Managing migration for growth 69

Chapter 6 Investing in people — **72**
From commitments to results — 73
Getting children into school — 76
Improving health — 78
Providing clean water and sanitation — 82
Protecting the very poorest — 84

Working internationally to tackle climate change

Chapter 7 Managing climate change — **90**
The climate is changing — 91
Climate change matters for development — 92
Working for an international solution — 93
Making the shift to cleaner energy — 96
Helping developing countries to adapt — 97

Creating an international system fit for the 21st century

Chapter 8 Reforming the international development system — **104**
The international system must change — 105
Collective action in a changing world: the United Nations — 106
Improving the international response to humanitarian crises — 108
Financing development: the International Financial Institutions — 110
Regional approaches to regional issues — 113
A new alliance for development: the European Union — 114
Holding each other to account — 117

What can you do? — 122

Glossary — 127

Endnotes — 128

foreword

Tony Blair, Prime Minister

Eliminating world poverty is in Britain's interests – and is one of the greatest moral challenges we face.

In 1997, the Labour Government established the Department for International Development, to underline our clear commitment to ending extreme poverty in the world. Since 1997, we have increased aid for developing countries by 140% in real terms, from £2.1 billion to £5.9 billion. In 2004, we set a clear timetable for us to meet the UN target of 0.7%, by 2013. And in 2005 we put development and Africa at the heart of our G8 Presidency.

Backed by enormous public support from the Make Poverty History coalition and the Live8 concerts, the Gleneagles G8 Summit in July 2005 agreed a comprehensive, detailed plan to fight poverty. This included plans to support an African Peacekeeping Force, provide universal access to AIDS treatment, and promote investment and infrastructure to create jobs for poor people.

G8 countries agreed to provide an extra US$50 billion a year in aid by 2010, and to double aid for Africa. And African leaders at Gleneagles agreed in return to draw up ambitious plans to tackle poverty, and to work to end corruption, bad governance and conflict.

This new White Paper on *Eliminating World Poverty* sets out how the UK will work with others to deliver on the promises we made last year. This will need an effort right across Government, to put our pledges into practice, to promote better governance across the world, to tackle the threat of climate change, and to create an international development system that is fit for purpose.

We are making real progress. This White Paper shows there are many success stories. But there is still a very long way to go. It will need continuing commitment, and continuing support from the British public, to achieve this. But if we work together, it can be done. There is no greater or more just cause facing us today.

Tony Blair

July 2006

preface
the challenge for our generation

Hilary Benn, Secretary of State for International Development

The scandal of poverty…

Today, over six billion members of the human family share our small and fragile planet. A human family that is more interdependent than at any other point in history. And a family that – for the first time – has the capacity to make sure that every one of its members is lifted out of poverty.

What people want and need is enough food to eat and water to drink. A roof over their heads, a job, a school for their children, and medicine and care when they are sick. The chance to live in peace, without fear of violence or war. And the opportunity to realise the potential in each and every one of us.

This is what development – at its best – has always been about. Development is not only about care for the poorest and the most vulnerable, or a helping hand when disaster strikes. Nor is it only about addressing the root causes of poverty, whether through aid or debt relief, or fairer trade and better governance. I believe, like the economist Amartya Sen, that development is above all about freedom. In his book *Development as Freedom,* Sen argues that millions upon millions of our human family are living imprisoned: by economic poverty, by political tyranny, by sickness and disease, by ignorance, and by oppression and violence. But now, we have the capacity to free our fellow human beings, once and for all, so that each one can enjoy freedom's 'thousand charms'.

The scandal is not only that so many lack the chance to fulfil their potential for want of an education, basic medical care or a functioning economy. Nor is it only that each day one in

six human beings has to live on less than one dollar or that 30,000 children die needlessly; or that each year half a million women still die in pregnancy or childbirth; or that we could give AIDS treatment to every single person in the world that needs it, but have not.

No, for me the greatest shame is that all this happens not in an age of famine and world war, but in an era of unprecedented plenty and potential, in a world eight times richer than it was 50 years ago.

…and what 2005 did about it.

2005 was the year in which Nelson Mandela addressed a packed Trafalgar Square and 250,000 people took to the streets of Edinburgh. In the UK, one in every six citizens supported the Make Poverty History campaign. Millions of people the world over watched the Live8 concerts and raised their voices, not just to demand justice, but to press for action to fight global poverty.

In doing so, they provided the most eloquent and inspiring response to the gloomy pessimists and the cynics who muttered that politics could not make a difference, that there was no point in trying, and that nothing would ever change no matter what we did.

Governments did change their policies and made new promises, most notably with the G8 at Gleneagles undertaking to: increase aid by US$50 billion a year by 2010, with US$25 billion of that to go to Africa; cancel debt worth another US$50 billion; and provide AIDS treatment to all who need it by 2010. Already we have seen progress on debt cancellation, increased aid, a new humanitarian fund and funding for AIDS. The UK has changed its approach too: doubling aid since 1997; committing for the first time ever to a timetable – 2013 – for giving 0.7% of Gross National Income in development aid; writing off 100% of the debt owed to us by some of the world's poorest nations; winning support for the International Finance Facility

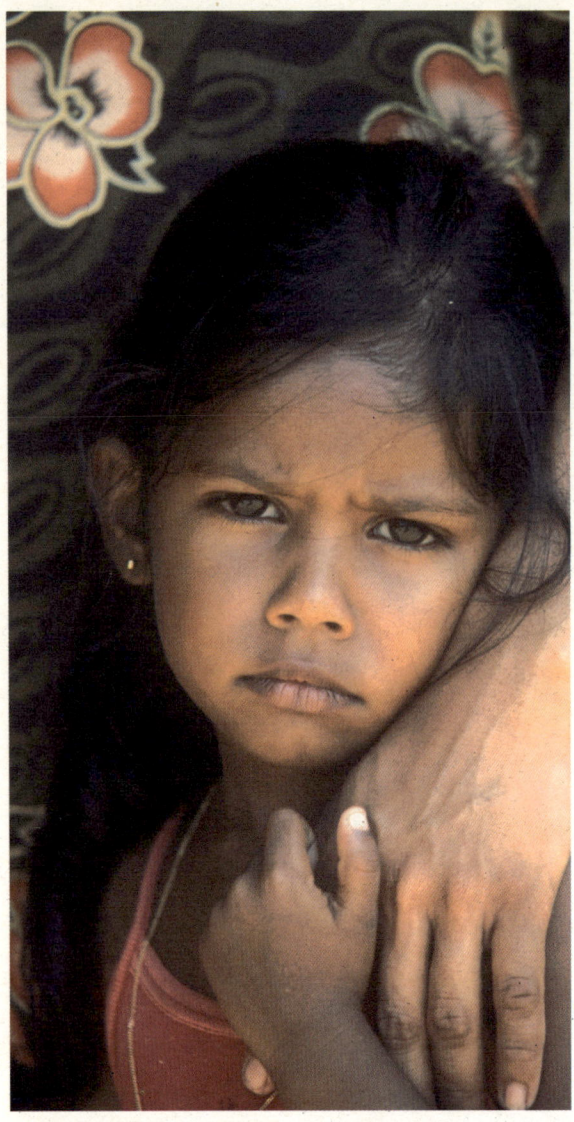

for Immunisation which aims to save the lives of 5 million human beings over the next decade; and making Africa a priority through our G8 and European Union presidencies.

True, by the end of the year, poverty had not been made history. Most poor people continued their lives in countries still far from achieving the Millennium Development Goals, and too many children had died – deaths that could have been prevented. It was not a moment for triumphalism, but it was a year that saw real progress. Things felt different, but only time – and what we do – will tell whether they really were.

So, now the challenge for the world's governments is to make good on these commitments – especially on trade where we have failed so far – and to prove that aid increases and debt relief really will make a difference. We have a double promise to fulfil: a promise to the world's poor not to let them down; and a promise to our own people that our aid will truly help those fighting for a more just tomorrow. This White Paper sets out what the UK will now do to make sure that these promises are fulfilled.

But 2005 represented more than just a change in governments' policy and spending. It was a recognition by the citizens of the world that we have all become more interconnected and more interdependent. It is no longer acceptable for the privileged few to turn their backs on the many. We can no longer claim that we did not know what was going on. Make Poverty History and the Global Call to Action Against Poverty represented both an acceptance of the responsibility that comes with this change and a belief that we can do something about it.

In a changing world…

If this belief is proved right, then it will not have come a moment too soon. Because every day that global poverty continues is a day too many.

But first, we should recognise that some things have changed for the better. Over the past 40 years, the proportion of people in developing countries who can read and write has risen from under half to nearly three-quarters. Average life expectancy has increased by around fifteen years, and there are 300 million more children now in school. Smallpox was eradicated just over a generation ago, and we are on the brink of doing the same with polio. Asia has seen a staggering reduction in poverty. China's success is not just good for its people. It has also helped lift others out of poverty across the continent, and provided opportunities for trade with other developing regions. The truth is that, in the right circumstances, development works. Aid works. Debt relief works. Things can change, and have changed, for the better.

But our world now stands at a crossroads. There are reasons for hope: the energy and politics of 2005, the power of economic development to change lives, the way that our technological and scientific ingenuity can be put at the service of the world's poor, the rapid growth of multilateralism over the past century, and a growing awareness that global co-operation is needed to match global interdependence.

But there are also causes for concern. Progress towards achieving the Millennium Development Goals is uneven, with the biggest challenge in Sub-Saharan Africa and South Asia. Women continue to be denied their rights. Over 40 million people are already living with HIV. Tuberculosis and malaria could become even greater killers as a result of the spread of HIV and of climate change. New 'flash epidemics' like avian flu or SARS could move through the world rapidly if they are not nipped in the bud.

A generation of teenagers is entering the workforce in developing economies. By 2010, 733 million more people will be of working age, compared to 50 million more in the rich world. Many of them will migrate – internally and abroad – in search of a better life. But, by 2030, two billion people could also be living in slums without access to healthcare, education or sanitation. If ways of earning a living aren't available to help this new generation to realise their dreams,

then their bitterness and anger at a world that has let them down could lead instead to political instability and radicalisation.

And other trends – rapid economic change, inequality, disease, and competition for natural resources – could all push developing countries further down the path to violent conflict.

But most important of all will be the challenge of managing our world sustainably and fairly. By the middle of this century, over 9 billion people will be sharing our planet; a half more than today. Meanwhile, the consumption of those of us already here – mainly in developed countries – is running at unsustainable levels. Many of the natural resources on which we all rely, and on which our economic development has always depended, are becoming seriously depleted.

Already, a third of the world's people live in countries which don't have enough water; by 2025, that proportion will rise to two thirds. Global fish stocks are running down faster than they can renew themselves. The world's land is under pressure from deforestation, unsustainable agricultural practices, groundwater depletion, and urban spread. As I write, oil prices are at their highest level ever.

Meanwhile, climate change is becoming the most serious and urgent problem the world faces. Unless we take radical action now, we face the shadow of a century of rising sea levels, droughts, hurricanes, heatwaves, glacial melting, floods, crop failures and forced migration. All of this will affect the poorest and most vulnerable people; the very people least responsible for the problem.

The scarcity of resources and climate change could stop development in its tracks. Yet on the other hand, there is the uncomfortable realisation that development, if not managed well, can itself make resources more scarce. The challenge, then, is to ensure that development is sustainable and also fair. Fighting on both of these fronts – the need to use resources wisely and within sustainable limits, whilst allowing the poorest countries and people a chance to prosper – will be at the very heart of 21st century development.

...global good governance...

In order to meet these global challenges, we will need to act globally more than ever. When we look at the principal institutions of multilateralism – the United Nations, the World Bank and International Monetary Fund, the World Trade Organisation, and the European Union – the chief characteristic they share is that they were all the result of the 1945 post-war settlement. They were, in other words, institutions built for a world very different from today's.

Back in 1945, the burning challenge of the day was to rebuild Europe and Japan and to avoid the new cold war becoming a third world war. If we were creating the multilateral system from scratch today, the foremost challenges in mind would be trade and investment, climate change and scarcity of resources, state failure, conflicts within states, the movement of people, international corruption and terrorism. So it is natural that we should look at the multilateral system critically, ask whether it is working, and be ready to help make it work better.

The European Union is also evolving swiftly. EU countries will account for the lion's share of the new aid commitments agreed last year at Gleneagles. Countries that were until recently recipients of aid have now, with accession to the EU, become donors. So it makes sense for the UK to work more closely with other European countries, both to influence their thinking and to make Europe's development effort much more effective.

Global good governance is not just about big organisations. It's also – just as importantly – about the framework of global governance to help create a safer world. One example of this is building capacity to deal with conflicts. Another is the UK's call for a new Arms Trade Treaty. Yet another is the need for greater co-operation in combating corruption and dealing at the global level with problems that can undermine governance in countries, such as illicit international markets for natural resources like minerals and timber.

...and good governance in countries will make all the difference.

Ultimately, it is within individual countries that poverty will be eliminated. Nation states are central to the change that is needed. The commitments made in 2005, in particular relating to Africa, represented a deal. A contract in which increased aid and debt relief were offered in return for a commitment to better governance.

Good governance and development are about people and governments of developing countries working out this deal for themselves. Each country needs to decide its own economic and social priorities, and the best people to hold governments to account are those who live in the country and are most affected by its decisions.

Whether states are effective or not – whether they are capable of helping business grow, and of delivering services to their citizens, and are accountable and responsive to them – is the single most important factor that determines whether or not successful development takes place. Good governance requires: capability – the extent to which government has the money, people, will and legitimacy to get things done; responsiveness – the degree to which government listens to what people want and acts on it; and accountability – the process by which people are able to hold government to account.

To achieve lasting improvements in living conditions for large numbers of people, the capacity and accountability of public institutions needs to be strengthened. That's why DFID already does so much to help developing countries build their capacity in areas like public financial management, police and civil service reform, and health and education. We will continue with this work and build on it. But we will also do much more at the grassroots end of political governance, working with organisations that train citizens' groups in budget monitoring to make sure that money is spent where it's supposed to be; increasing our support to a free press and media in developing countries; and offering much more support in areas like elections, human rights, parliaments and trade unions.

I am determined to ensure that our rising aid budget is used for the purpose for which it is given – helping to lift people out of poverty. We have to show results. That's why we will make a careful assessment of the best way to do this in each country and vary the way we give our aid accordingly. And we will be resolute in the fight against corruption.

In the end, governance – from the global right down to the village level – is about

people and their relationships, one with another, more than it is about formal institutions. What makes the biggest difference to the quality of governance is active involvement by citizens – the thing we know as politics.

This, more than anything, lay at the heart of Make Poverty History last year. It's the only thing that can in the long run transform the quality of decision making in developing countries, and the effectiveness of states. It's why DFID's partners are not just governments but also people with the energy, courage and vision to make poverty history in their own countries.

And politics is also what all of us will rely on here in the UK to sustain support for international development. When citizens get involved in any one of a hundred ways, it puts life into politics. It shows how we can turn our burning hope for a better world into helping the poorest billion people on our planet to change their own lives for the better. As Nelson Mandela said in Trafalgar Square last year "Sometimes it falls upon a generation to be great." It is up to us to accept that responsibility and do what needs to be done.

Hil Benn

Pierre Labrie / Still Pictures

This White Paper is about delivering the promises made in 2005 and responding to the four big challenges for international development.

First and foremost, the fight against poverty cannot be won without good governance. We need to help governments and citizens make politics work for the poor. And we need to make global governance better, because the international economy affects what happens in each country.

Second, we must help countries – especially those at risk of falling ever further behind the rest of the world – do better in ensuring security, achieving sustainable growth, and delivering health and education for all.

Third, if we do not act urgently, the threat posed by climate change will derail development.

And finally, because no country can do this alone, we must make the international system fit for the 21st century.

To this end, over the next five years, the UK will, in summary:

…deliver our promises…

1 Fulfil the commitments we made in 2005, and work through the G8, United Nations, and European Union to ensure that our partners do the same.

2 Increase our development budget to 0.7% of Gross National Income by 2013 and, working with others, press ahead with innovative financing mechanisms like the International Finance Facility and an Air Solidarity Levy.

3 Concentrate our development assistance on countries with the largest numbers of poor people, particularly in sub-Saharan Africa and South Asia; and on fragile states, especially those vulnerable to conflict.

4 Make sure that our wider policies, as well as aid, support development; and work with the European Union, G8 and others, including large developing countries such as China, India and South Africa, to create an international environment that promotes development.

5 Double our funding for science and technology research, including efforts to find better drugs, and new technologies for water treatment, agriculture and to manage climate change.

…..help to build states that work for poor people…

6 Put support for good governance at the centre of what we do, focusing on state capability, responsiveness and accountability, working in particular with citizens, civil society groups, parliamentarians and the media. Adopt a new 'quality of governance' assessment to guide the way in which we give UK aid, and launch a new £100 million Governance and Transparency Fund.

7 Tackle corruption; follow up the Extractive Industries Transparency Initiative with further steps to bring greater transparency into public revenues and procurement; and work internationally to tackle bribery, corruption and money laundering.

8 Decide how to provide UK aid based on partner countries' commitment to reduce poverty, uphold human rights and international obligations, improve financial management, promote good governance and transparency, and fight corruption.

...help people have security, incomes, and public services...

9 Work to help states promote peace and security. Where states are unable to protect their citizens, we will work with our international partners to prevent, manage and respond to conflict.

10 Promote rapid growth by supporting private sector development and employment, investing in infrastructure and agriculture, and working for international trade rules that maximise the opportunities for the poorest countries.

11 Commit at least half of all future UK direct support for developing countries to public services, to get children into school, improve healthcare, fight HIV and AIDS, provide more clean water and sanitation, and offer social protection; and agree ten year commitments with developing countries to do this.

12 Seek to make sure that growth is equitable, and that natural resources are used sustainably.

...work internationally to tackle climate change...

13 Work for international agreements on climate change that stabilise greenhouse gas levels in the atmosphere, enable developing countries to grow, create incentives and generate investment for clean energy, and help poor countries to adapt to the impact.

14 Work with developing countries to make sure that they are fully involved in future international discussions on climate change, and provide international support to help developing countries adapt.

...and create an international system fit for the 21st century.

15 Work with others, and use our resources and influence, to push for change in the international system. This means: reform of the UN; a more effective UN-led system to deal with humanitarian crises; more

responsive international financial institutions; supporting the growing roles of regional organisations such as the African Development Bank and the African Union; and a strong focus on merit-based appointments, and greater accountability to developing countries.

16 Work more closely with European partners to promote development.

17 Push for the Organisation of Economic Co-operation and Development's Development Assistance Committee to monitor and hold donors to account on their development commitments, and to work more closely with new non-OECD donors such as India and China..

Full details of our proposals are set out in the following chapters.

delivering our promises

chapter 1
delivering the promises of 2005

> **The promises of 2005 have the potential to change the lives of a billion men, women and children.**
>
> **Keeping those promises, in a rapidly changing world, is our priority.**

The case for development...

1.1 Poverty is about people. One in every six human beings – one billion people – lives on less than US$1 a day.[1] Poverty for these men, women and children means not having enough food to eat, no clean water, no place in school, a mother dying needlessly, living in fear and violence, and little opportunity for a better life.

1.2 In the fight against global poverty, 2005 saw rich and poor countries make promises that will change people's lives. These promises were made because people demanded them and leaders listened. They demonstrated that international politics can work in the interests of the poorest.

> ### What is poverty?
> **"Poverty is like heat: you cannot see it, you can only feel it; to know poverty you have to go through it."**
> Saying from Adaboya, Ghana

Marching to make poverty history

"As a veteran of all the major campaigns to fight poverty... the Make Poverty History campaign was different. Walking 25 miles a day for two weeks to link the two British G8 venues of Birmingham and Gleneagles, we found enormous public support and interest everywhere we went. The white tape decked countless towns and villages. A mountain of cards and letters and a quarter of a million demonstrators awaited us in Edinburgh. Our hopes were high that this time we simply couldn't be ignored. The public have spoken and we will continue until we've seen it through."

Merryn Hellier, Member of the Jubilee Debt Campaign, Hereford, 2006

1.3 The promises made in 2005 were part of a deal. The Commission for Africa set out its proposals.[2] At Gleneagles, African leaders committed themselves and their people to lead their own development by improving governance, upholding the rule of law, and using their resources to fight poverty.[3] In turn, the G8 and European Union (EU) promised to provide an additional US$50 billion for development – increasing health and education provision, tackling HIV and AIDS, and promoting economic growth – and to improve the way that aid was spent. They promised to cancel debt, improve access to international markets, help poor countries suffering from conflict or humanitarian emergencies, and tackle international corruption and climate change.

1.4 There has been progress over the last year. Twenty-one countries have already had all of their debt to the International Monetary Fund (IMF) cancelled. Nineteen countries – fifteen in Africa - have had their debts to the World Bank's International Development Association cancelled. The UK, with others, has launched the International Finance Facility for Immunisation (IFFIm). This has the potential to save the lives of 5 million children over the next ten years and another 5 million after that. The Global Plan to Stop TB (tuberculosis) and the Global Strategic Plan to Roll Back Malaria have been launched. The UK has helped establish an Infrastructure Consortium and an Investment Climate Facility for Africa. The UN Convention Against Corruption has come into force – the UK ratified it in February 2006. The Extractive Industries Transparency Initiative (EITI) is now being implemented in over twenty countries. Twenty-six countries have signed up to the African Peer Review Mechanism, thirteen reviews are under way and Ghana, Kenya and Rwanda have completed their reviews. The UN Peacebuilding Commission and UN Central Emergency Response Fund have been established. And the EU has agreed to provide Euros 300 million to support African peacekeeping efforts.

1.5 Much more remains to be done. To sustain this new momentum in the fight against poverty, it will be essential to monitor progress. In the UK we have set milestones for action and will continue to publish updates so that Parliament and civil society can hold us to account. The G8 will publish a progress report this year. The new Africa Progress Panel will focus international political attention on Africa and track progress against the commitments made in 2005. As agreed at Gleneagles, the Africa Partnership Forum – which brings together African countries and their international partners – will also continue to monitor progress annually. The Development Assistance Committee

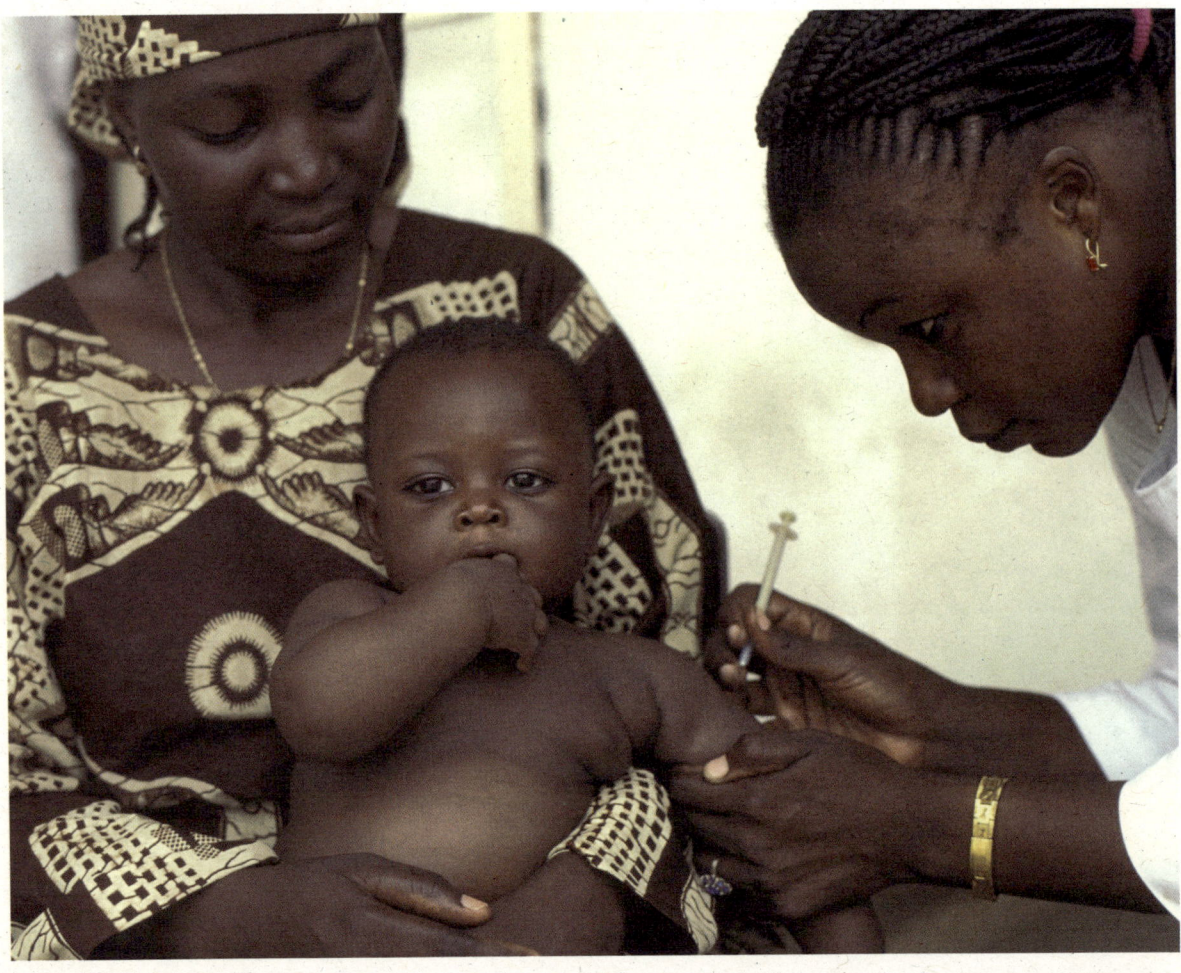

2005 – the promises

The G8 Summit agreed to:

- Double aid to Africa by 2010 and give an extra US$50 billion a year globally.
- Cancel the debts owed by some of the world's poorest countries to the International Monetary Fund, World Bank and African Development Bank. This will be worth over US$50 billion when fully implemented, and 90% will go to Africa.
- Write off US$18 billion of Nigeria's debt, the biggest ever single debt deal for an African country.
- Uphold the principle that developing countries should decide their own economic policies to support their own development plans, for which they should be accountable to their own people.
- Get as close as possible to universal access to AIDS treatments by 2010.
- Support treatment and bed nets to fight malaria, aiming to save the lives of over 600,000 children every year.
- Fund the eradication of polio from the world.
- Ensure that by 2015 all children have access to free good quality education, and to basic health care free where a country chooses to provide it.
- Help the African Union to set up a Standby Force as part of the 2004 G8 commitment to train 75,000 troops for peacekeeping by 2010.
- Support early ratification of the UN Convention Against Corruption and find ways of recovering stolen assets.
- Implement effective controls over the transfer of small arms and light weapons.
- Implement a Plan of Action on Climate Change to speed up access by developing countries to low carbon energy and improve their resilience to climate change.

The EU agreed to:

- Set a new average EU aid target of 0.56% of Gross National Income by 2010 (doubling aid to US$80 billion) and 0.7% of Gross National Income by 15 EU Member States by 2015.
- Adopt a new EU development policy with the central aim of reducing poverty.
- Implement a new EU Africa Strategy to support Africa to reach the Millennium Development Goals.

The UN World Summit agreed to:

- Recommit all UN member states to the Millennium Development Goals and other international targets including those agreed at the World Summit on Sustainable Development.
- Establish a new UN Peacebuilding Commission.
- Endorse the concept of "Responsibility to Protect" when states fail to protect their people from genocide, war crimes, ethnic cleansing or crimes against humanity.
- Establish a global humanitarian fund (the Central Emergency Response Fund).
- Re-affirm that managing natural resources sustainably is essential for development.
- Establish a UN Human Rights Council.

The World Trade Organisation talks agreed to work to:

- End all agricultural export subsidies by 2013, with substantial progress by 2010.
- Move, in principle, towards duty free and quota free market access for all products from the poorest countries by 2008.
- End cotton export subsidies by 2006.
- Increase substantially trade-related assistance, including a UK pledge to increase its support to £100 million per year by 2010.

of the Organisation for Economic Co-operation and Development (OECD DAC) and the EU are monitoring financial commitments. And the African Monitor – launched by the Archbishop of Cape Town – will help African civil society hold their governments to account.

1.6 This White Paper sets out how the UK Government will work with others to deliver the promises of 2005. It builds on the international development White Papers published in 1997 and 2000, and is framed by the International Development Act of 2002. Promoting sustainable development is a Strategic International Priority for the UK as set out in the Government's 2006 White Paper 'Active Diplomacy for a Changing World'.[4] We believe that eliminating world poverty is not only morally right, but that it will also create a safer, more prosperous world for us all.

Poverty is falling, but progress is uneven…

1.7 In the last two decades there has been dramatic progress in reducing poverty. Thanks to rapid economic growth in Asia the number of people across the world living on less than US$1 a day is set to halve by 2015.[5] There are now over 75 million more children in primary school than there were in 1990, and the gap between the number of boys and girls in education is slowly closing.[6] There are ten times as many people receiving AIDS treatment as there were in 2000.[7]

1.8 But progress has been uneven. On current trends, many of the Millennium Development Goals (MDGs) will not be met.[8] AIDS killed over 3 million people last year.[9] Half a million women still die in pregnancy or childbirth each year. And while death rates of children under the age of five have been dropping, every day around 30,000 children still die from preventable causes.[10]

The UK will

- Fulfil the commitments we made in 2005.

- Increase our development budget to 0.7% of Gross National Income by 2013.

- Work with others to press ahead with innovative ways of raising finance for development, like the International Finance Facility and an Air Solidarity Levy.

- Work with the G8, Africa Progress Panel, Africa Partnership Forum, UN, World Bank, EU, OECD DAC and civil society to monitor progress and ensure that developed and developing countries live up to their commitments.

Where do the poorest people live?

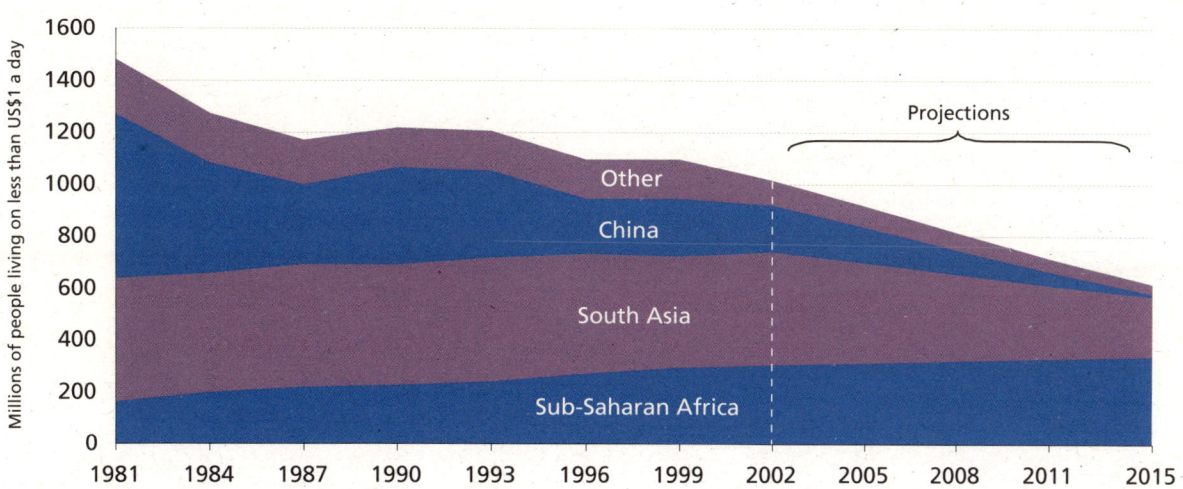

Source: World Bank Development Indicators 2006

1.9 Most of the improvements have been in Asia, particularly in East Asia. Some countries in sub-Saharan Africa are making progress, but the region as a whole will not meet any of the MDGs; and South Asia is off-track on education, health, water and sanitation.[11] Across both regions, the spread of AIDS, malaria, tuberculosis and other diseases continues to present a major challenge. Progress has also been slow in other regions, such as Latin America and Central Asia – but the absolute numbers of poor people there remain low compared to South Asia and sub-Saharan Africa. On current trends, by 2015, over 90% of the world's poor will live in sub-Saharan African and South Asia.[12]

1.10 Progress is slowest on the MDGs that depend most heavily on improving the status of women and girls. Gender discrimination is not only unjust but holds back economic growth and sustainable development.[13] Around a third of people living on less than US$1 a day in sub-Saharan Africa are chronically poor – they experience poverty most or all of their lives. Trapped in this way, they die of easily preventable causes and pass on only poverty to their children.[14] They have no way out and targeted assistance is needed to help them.

1.11 One third of the world's poor people live in 'fragile states'.[15] Fragile states include those that have collapsed, such as Somalia, or have difficulties controlling their territory, as does Afghanistan. They may be in conflict, or recovering from conflict, such as Sudan, Nepal and Angola. Climate change, energy insecurity, scarcity of resources, population growth and migration could increase the

Learning to tackle exclusion

Sita is 11 and lives in a hut next to the railway line in Patna, India. She belongs to the Musaha community, a low status caste. Fewer than 1% of Musaha women can read and write. When Sita went to primary school the other children called her names and refused to sit next to her. The teacher said she needed a bath and threw her satchel out of the classroom. Sita was so upset, she refused to go back. Her parents hadn't been to school and were too shy to go and talk to the teachers, so Sita stayed at home looking after her younger brothers and sisters. But Sita's life changed when a charity set up a class for girls. Now she is learning to read and write and wants to go back to mainstream school.

number of fragile states. By 2010, half of the world's poorest people could be living in such places, as more successful countries and regions leave them behind.[16] Working in these countries is difficult, but high levels of poverty and the threat of conflict mean they deserve significantly more international attention.

The UK will

- Concentrate our resources on poor countries in sub-Saharan Africa and in South Asia.
- Work more in those fragile states that receive less aid overall in relation to the number of poor people they have and which are most off-track on the MDGs.
- Work in the middle income countries that have the largest numbers of poor people and the greatest regional and global influence on development; and maintain links with others (including through the EU) in order to help them avoid slipping back to low income status.[17]
- Give greater priority to our work in support of gender equality and women's rights.
- Continue to meet the development needs and promote the self sufficiency of the UK's Overseas Territories.[18]

Making progress against the 2005 commitments…

1.12 The promises of 2005 must be kept in a world that is changing rapidly. This makes the task of helping people to improve their lives all the more difficult. These global trends will bring new opportunities. Fast-growing countries like China, India and South Africa are generating trade and investment in other developing countries. But these trends will also pose significant challenges, such as climate change, especially for the poorest countries. It is therefore essential to work with developing countries to manage these global challenges and to help them respond. Our development assistance and other international policies must work in tandem to promote development. And we must build on the huge wave of support in 2005 – from the

public, media, charities, faith groups and trade unions – that pushed governments to take action.

1.13 As this White Paper sets out, eliminating poverty means tackling four main challenges.

1.14 First, good governance is fundamental. Governance is about the *capability* of governments to get things done, how they *respond* to the needs and rights of their citizens, and how, in turn, people can hold their governments to *account*. In short, governance is about politics – the way in which citizens and government relate to each other.

1.15 Developing countries must keep the promises they have made on governance. But the international community must also do more to tackle the international causes of poor governance. Chapters 2 and 3 set out what developing countries, the UK and others need to do to achieve this.

1.16 Second, there needs to be rapid progress on the commitments made by developing countries and the international community to provide peace and security, encourage economic growth, and invest in the most important public services.

1.17 Additional resources will be essential for this. At the UN World Summit, developing countries promised to make full use of their own resources for development. Encouraging faster economic growth is the only way to reduce dependence on aid. But even with this growth, the poorest countries will not be able to generate sufficient resources over the next ten years to meet their needs for investment and public services.

1.18 We must, therefore, ensure that the international community delivers the US$50 billion increase in aid promised by 2010. Nearly 80% of this was promised by members of the EU. Innovative financing, such as the International Finance Facility and the Air Solidarity Levy, could help raise these resources more quickly. But the extra aid must also be spent well. In the past, aid has been unpredictable and often given for commercial or political reasons. This has made it difficult for poor countries to make long term plans. Aid has improved significantly in recent years but could be better. Developing countries must now make ambitious plans that international partners can support. And international

Science changes lives

Using science in the fight against poverty: Managing global challenges requires investment in science, technological advances and innovation. Developing country governments need access to the best international expertise. And with the right networks, scientists in developing countries can encourage governments to use their skills to help the poorest people. The UK is investing in partnerships between researchers, international companies and people in developing countries – such as community groups, the media and private sector – to exploit science to fight poverty.

Tackling problems through research: Whiteflies and the viruses they carry affect the lives of 15 million people who tend 20 million hectares of food crops in some of the poorest countries. The UK has helped bring together more than 100 agricultural research organisations, universities, scientists, non-governmental organisations, and farming groups from 50 countries. The collaboration led to the development of virus-resistant crops and policies that prevented the collapse of major food-crops in over 30 countries.

Public-Private Partnerships – joining the fight against malaria: Malaria kills more than three African children each minute.[19] The Medicines for Malaria Venture, a public-private partnership, has brought together academic institutions and pharmaceutical companies to research anti-malarial drugs, some of which are due to be approved and licensed in the next few years.

partners must transform the way aid is allocated and delivered. The promises made in 2005 on aid mean that it will now be possible – for the first time – to make the long term commitments necessary to fight poverty. These issues are explored in chapters 4, 5, 6 and 8.

1.19 Third, climate change, together with natural resource depletion, is the biggest threat facing the world. Climate change is a huge challenge which is set to put unprecedented pressure on resources and people in developing countries. Developing countries will need support to adapt to the impact of climate change and urgent action is needed to cut emissions and prevent dangerous levels of climate change in the future. These challenges, and what needs to be done, are covered in Chapter 7.

1.20 And fourth, we need effective international organisations if we are to win the fight against poverty. The following chapters set out how the UN, World Bank, EU and other international organisations can help developing countries tackle poverty and deal with the wider challenges facing them. And in chapter 8, we set out the UK's views on reform of the international development system.

1.21 As this White Paper shows, development can make a difference to the lives of the poorest billion people in the world. Developing countries and their international partners know what needs to be done. 2005 has given us the best opportunity to make sure that everybody, everywhere has the chance to live a better life. We must not squander it.

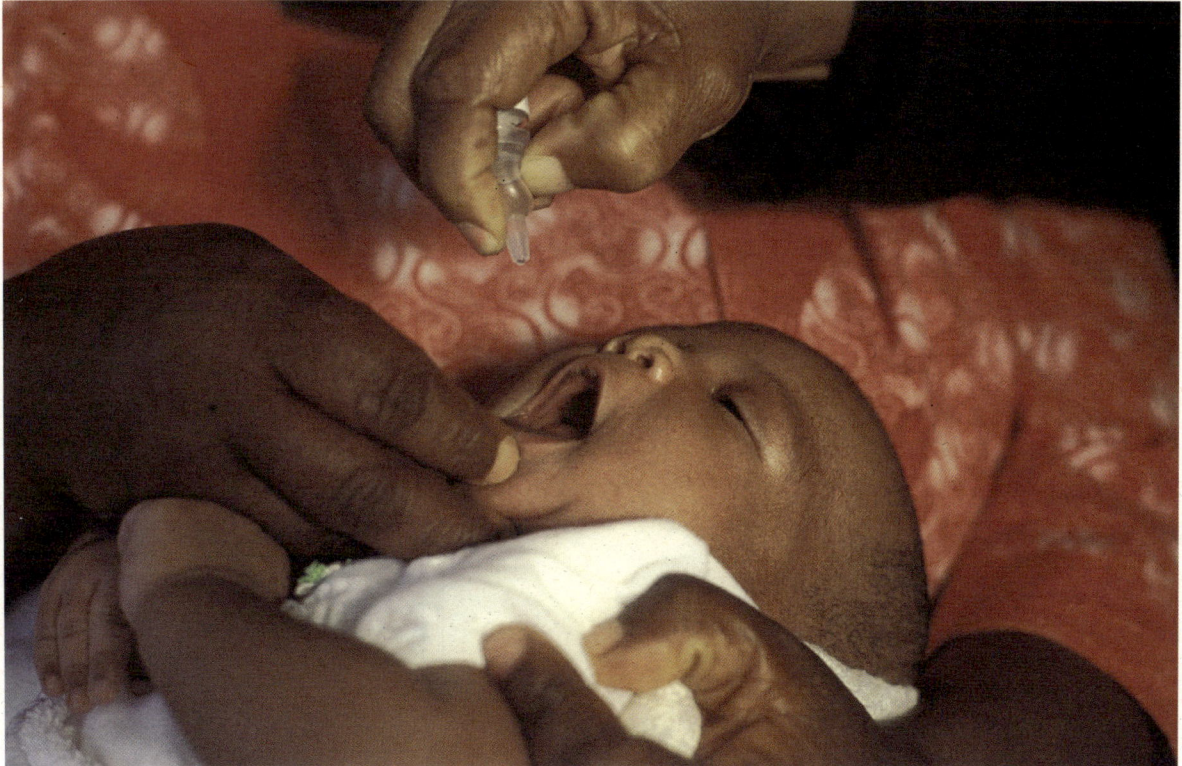

Aid works

Aid helps reduce poverty by increasing economic growth, improving governance and increasing access to public services. In Mozambique, after the war in the mid 1990s, aid – totalling more than 50% of national income a year - helped increase the growth rate to an astonishing 12%. Poverty fell from around 70% in 1996 to under 55% by 2003. In Rwanda, in the ten years since the genocide, aid – over 15% of national income a year – helped reduce poverty from 70% in 1994 to under 60% in 2001.[20] In Africa as a whole, the situation would be worse without aid – economic growth would have been around 1% lower between 1973 and 2001.[21] And contrary to popular belief, aid reduces the risk of money leaving the country, because it encourages people in developing countries to keep their wealth at home rather than abroad.[22]

Aid is helping countries make progress towards the MDGs.[23] Aid has helped eradicate smallpox and – soon – polio. In Uganda, aid made it possible for the Government to offer free health care, which doubled the number of people visiting clinics and the number of children immunised.

And, as the Commission for Africa showed, aid can help improve the way a country is governed. Ghana, which used to experience regular coups, is now a stable democracy with a growing economy. Aid, supporting the Government's poverty reduction plan, helped to achieve this.

So aid works – but the amount of aid and the way it is used has a significant impact on how effective it is.

Debt relief works

Debt relief (which is a form of aid) provides reliable and predictable resources for developing countries. Twenty-nine countries increased their spending on the MDGs from about US$6 billion in 1999 to US$13 billion in 2005 because of the Heavily Indebted Poor Countries (HIPC) Initiative.[24] The UK supports and is financing our share of 100% multilateral and bilateral debt cancellation for low income countries that are committed to using the savings to fight poverty. In 2005, the G8 announced the Multilateral Debt Relief Initiative, which will write off 100% of all remaining debt owed by HIPCs to the IMF, World Bank and African Development Fund. In total, this could be worth over US$50 billion for 45 countries. The additional resources available from this have already helped Zambia to announce an end to fees for basic health care in rural areas.

The UK will

- Help partner countries to deal with the global trends that have the greatest impact on development.

- Work with others, including the G8, UN, EU and other partners, such as China, India and South Africa, to create an international environment that promotes development.

- Report annually to Parliament on the effectiveness of UK policy and expenditure in helping to reduce poverty and support sustainable development, in line with the International Development (Reporting and Transparency) Bill currently before Parliament.

- Push for the full implementation and financing of the Heavily Indebted Poor Countries Initiative.

- Work towards 100% multilateral and bilateral debt cancellation for all the poorest countries that are committed to using savings to reduce poverty.

- Double our research funding by 2010, focusing on achieving the MDGs.

delivering our promises

helping to build states that work for poor people

chapter 2
building effective states and better governance

Effective states are central to development. They protect people's rights and provide security, economic growth and services like education and health care.

Building better governance takes time and has to come from within each country, but international partners can help.

This means we need to work not just with governments, but also with citizens and civil society.

Good governance is essential to reduce poverty …

2.1 People want to be governed well, and to have a say in what happens in their lives. They want to be safe. They want the chance to earn a decent living for themselves and their families. And they want to be treated fairly by their government and public officials. These aspirations are enshrined in the Universal Declaration of Human Rights, and the Millennium Declaration of 2000. But the reality for many people in poor countries is very different.

2.2 Effective states and better governance are essential to combat poverty. States which respect civil liberties and are accountable to their citizens are more stable, which in turn means they are more

A tale of two states

Tanzania is an increasingly effective state. It has a stable government committed to economic growth and reducing poverty, and a national plan known as Mkukuta which the UK and other international partners are supporting. Over the last decade the Government has improved public finances, and strengthened local government. It is improving the conditions for business and is taking action on corruption. The result? The economy has grown 6% a year since 2000. There is less corruption. The proportion of children in primary school has leapt from 58% in 2000 to 95% in 2005. And infant mortality rates are down by a third since 1999.

Zimbabwe is a failing state. The ruling party used draconian measures to hold on to power. Human rights are abused. The rule of law has been undermined. Commercial farming was destroyed by drastic land reforms, and economic mismanagement has led to sharp rises in public borrowing. The private sector has lost confidence. The result? The economy has shrunk by 40% in the past seven years. Inflation has soared over 1,000% and unemployment to 70%. Food is in short supply and the international community is now helping feed the population. Public services have almost collapsed. Huge numbers of Zimbabweans have left the country and, for those who remain, life expectancy has fallen to 34 years. Four in five people are living below the national poverty line.

likely to attract investment and generate long term economic growth.[1] They can also cope better with calamities. Famines, for example, are less likely where there is a free media, because the press creates pressure on governments to provide relief.[2] Unless governance improves, poor people will continue to suffer from a lack of security, public services and economic opportunities. The contrast between Tanzania and Zimbabwe over the past decade is striking.

2.3 So what is good governance? Good governance is not just about government. It is also about political parties, parliament, the judiciary, the media, and civil society. It is about how citizens, leaders and public institutions relate to each other in order to make change happen. Elections and democracy are an important part of the equation, but equally important is the way government goes about the business of governing. Good governance requires three things:

- State capability – the extent to which leaders and governments are able to get things done.

- Responsiveness – whether public policies and institutions respond to the needs of citizens and uphold their rights.

- Accountability – the ability of citizens, civil society and the private sector to scrutinise public institutions and governments and hold them to account. This includes, ultimately, the opportunity to change leaders by democratic means.

Understanding good governance

Capability means having the ability to perform certain functions….	Responsiveness means taking account of citizens' aspirations and needs…	Accountability means being answerable for what is done…
✓ Providing political stability and security.	✓ Providing ways for people to say what they think and need.	✓ Offering citizens opportunities to check the laws and decisions made by government, parliaments or assemblies.
✓ Setting good rules and regulations.	✓ Implementing policies that meet the needs of the poor.	Encouraging a free media and freedom of faith and association.
Creating the conditions for investment and trade, and promoting growth in jobs and incomes.	Using public finances to benefit the poor – for example to encourage growth and provide services.	✓ Respecting human rights and making sure the 'rule of law', is upheld, for example by an independent judiciary.
Managing public finances and putting government policies into practice effectively.	✓ Providing public goods and services in ways that reduce discrimination and allow all citizens – including women, disabled people and ethnic minorities – to benefit.	✓ Providing regular opportunities to change leaders in peaceful ways.
✓ Making sure government departments and services meet people's needs.		
Keeping borders secure and helping people move safely and legally.		

2.4 All three characteristics are needed to make states more effective, to tackle poverty and to improve people's lives. For example, there is no guarantee that a more capable health ministry will automatically focus on the diseases killing the poorest people unless it is responsive and accountable. The UK will now make it a priority to help our developing country partners improve governance on all three fronts.

Improving governance…

2.5 Significant improvements in governance can take place. Botswana, Ghana and Tanzania have strengthened their public institutions in recent years. Rwanda, Mozambique, Vietnam and Cambodia have successfully rebuilt their countries after devastating conflicts. And East Asian countries, such as Malaysia and South

Successful states – the East Asian experience

East Asian countries have made remarkable progress in raising living standards. A sense of national purpose has helped in this. Political leaders saw common interests between the citizen and the state, and built confidence in government's ability to maintain security, protect savings, promote investment and deliver better services.

Malaysia is a good example. Political leaders implemented policies to address economic inequalities faced by the largest ethnic group, but made sure domestic minorities and foreign investors were not excluded. Regional economic growth created new opportunities. And aid played a role in building government capability and providing access to technical knowledge.

Korea, have changed the lives of millions of their citizens.

2.6 In most cases, strong political leadership, economic growth, and a vibrant private sector were the main factors encouraging change. A growing middle class, more educated citizens, and a greater willingness by civil society and media to speak out pushed political leaders to improve the performance of the state. In some cases, the better off members of society led the demand for better governance. Businesses and trade unions demanded better rules and regulation. Professionals pressed for a more open media and the rule of law. People called for better representation by political parties in exchange for the taxes they paid.[3]

2.7 Accountability is at the heart of how change happens. Where accountability is good, audit institutions and parliamentary committees scrutinise the way government bodies spend their money and what they achieve. Courts help prevent abuse of office. And beyond the formal structures of the state, civil society organisations give citizens power, help poor people get their voices heard, and demand more from politicians and government.[4]

2.8 But some countries struggle to improve governance. Sometimes this is due to grievances and conflict – as has recently been the case in Palestine, Nepal and Sudan. On other occasions, it is because states are undermined by self-serving leaders who siphon off huge personal wealth from natural resources such as oil and diamonds. Sierra Leone, Angola and the Democratic Republic of Congo (DRC) have all suffered this 'natural resource curse'.[5] In many of these instances, corruption, unaccountable elites, patronage and ethnic divisions have distorted the political process.

2.9 Governance is influenced by what happens in the region, by international organisations and standards, and by the views of other countries and international partners. For example, peer reviews by the African Union (AU) and its New Partnership for Africa's Development (NEPAD) are beginning to show how governance can improve. But change takes time and outsiders cannot impose models. People and governments in developing countries have to choose better governance for themselves. Political parties, civil servants, journalists, trade unions,

businesses, faith and other civil society groups must determine the future of their countries. This is about politics. Politics determines how resources are used and policies are made. And politics determines who benefits. In short, good governance is about good politics.

The UK will use its aid to support good governance...

2.10 The UK Government has a responsibility to make sure that UK aid money is used for the purpose for which it is intended. We take this very seriously. In deciding how to provide assistance to developing country partners, we will in future consider three principles:

- Is there a commitment to reduce poverty?

- Is there a commitment to uphold human rights and international obligations?

- Is there a commitment to improve public financial management, promote good governance and transparency, and fight corruption?

2.11 To answer these questions, we will look at a government's record and its plans: are people's rights being respected, is spending on public services going up, are efforts being made to tackle social exclusion, is economic policy promoting growth, and are public finances well managed? Answering these questions will mean understanding the underlying politics and governance. We will use a new 'quality of governance' assessment to help us monitor whether governance is getting better or worse. We will do such assessments with others where possible, for example with the EU and World Bank.

2.12 Where governance is relatively good and improving, the UK will consider the use of direct budget support in order to back our partners' plans to fight poverty and increase spending on public services like health and education.[6] In these countries, our aid will be long term, predictable, and delivered through the country's own systems – because this delivers the best results for the least cost.[7] But even in these circumstances,

direct budget support must be accompanied by continuing efforts to improve the management of public finances, to build the capability of government to provide services, and to ensure citizens are able to hold governments to account. Wherever possible, we will work with other international partners to co-ordinate assistance – for example through joint plans or joint financing agreements – to reduce the burden on developing country partners.

2.13 In other cases, where governance is not so good – where the commitment to reduce poverty is weaker or where the risk of corruption is greater – we will still provide aid, sometimes budget support, but differently. Fragile states often lack the capacity to reduce poverty but, paradoxically, have an even greater need to deliver public services. Consequently, they also need long term, predictable, well co-ordinated assistance to improve government systems. But, in these cases, the UK will restrict how our money can be used. For example, we might: limit our aid to specific programmes that meet the needs of the poor; use basic services grants to direct aid to services like education and health; channel funds through ring-fenced accounts; set up implementation units outside government; or use independent and more frequent monitoring and auditing arrangements. In all cases, we will also invest in efforts to improve the long term capability, responsiveness and accountability of public institutions.

2.14 Where the government is simply not committed to helping its citizens, we will still use our aid to help poor people and to promote long term improvements in governance. But we will do this by working outside the government, and with international agencies like the UN and civil society organisations.

2.15 Where circumstances deteriorate – or improve – the UK will re-assess governance, our partners' commitment to the three principles and, where necessary, change the way we provide aid.

The UK will

- Adopt a new 'quality of governance' assessment to monitor governance and our partners' commitment to fighting poverty. The assessment will be done as part of our published Country Assistance Plans, or more frequently if necessary. It will be based on discussions with partner governments, civil society and other international partners.

- Use this assessment of 'quality of governance', as well as commitment to the three principles – reducing poverty; upholding human rights and international obligations; and improving public financial management, promoting good governance and transparency, and fighting corruption – to make choices about the way in which we give UK aid.

- In partner countries, help improve the capability of state institutions and strengthen accountability to the poor.

- Support the African Peer Review Mechanism launched by the New Partnership for Africa's Development to help partners improve governance.

International partners can help…

2.16 It is difficult to build better governance on all fronts at the same time. In states recovering from conflict, for example, it is important to create the conditions for security and justice. But sometimes providing basic services quickly may be more important. After the 1994 genocide, the Rwandan Government rapidly opened primary schools to show their commitment to educating children from all ethnic groups.

2.17 The UK has a strong record in working with developing countries to improve the capability of public institutions. 'Technical assistance' – often comprising specialist staff and training – offers new ideas and ways of working. Such support only works well when the institutions themselves want change and are ready to lead reform. Where there is strong leadership, for example in Rwanda it is possible for significant change to take place. As with financial aid, we believe technical assistance should be provided through government systems so that developing countries can design and manage it to meet their needs. And donors should pool technical assistance funds to improve co-ordination and reduce administrative burdens.

2.18 It is essential that international partners avoid doing things that undermine a country's capability. For example, some AIDS projects have recruited professional staff from government health services which are already struggling to provide health care. Or in fragile states, such as Afghanistan, giving aid only through non-governmental organisations (NGOs) or private contractors can actually hold back the process of building the capability of the state.

2.19 Consulting people improves government policy. Involving citizens and asking them what they want leads to better public services. International partners can encourage this. For example, the UK is helping countries to analyse the social impacts of policies, and to monitor and evaluate poverty reduction programmes.

How UK aid has helped Rwanda and elsewhere

The UK has provided substantial budget support and other assistance to Rwanda since the genocide in 1994 (which destroyed the house above). Public service reform is strengthening ways of managing staff and performance. This is helping local government to improve health and education. Land reform is paving the way for agricultural development and investment. The National Institute for Statistics is reviewing progress against the national Poverty Reduction Strategy. Rwanda's Revenue Authority has reduced paperwork for businesses and increased tax collection from 9% of gross domestic product in 1998 to 15% in 2005. The result? Rwanda's economy has grown by over 10% a year over the past decade. Spending on programmes to reduce poverty has increased. Poverty dropped from 70% in 1994 to 60% in 2002. Primary school enrolment has steadily climbed to 94%. Mother and infant death rates are falling. Nevertheless, there are challenges. Maintaining political stability is important but so too is allowing space for different political views and freedom of expression.

Other examples of UK support include:

- Improving tax agencies and systems. In Zambia and Mozambique UK technical assistance and funding has helped raise revenue rates significantly. In Uganda, reforms led to a 35% rise in tax revenues. These taxes are helping to fund poverty reduction programmes.

- Improving how public finances are managed. In places like Tanzania, Ghana, Pakistan, Bangladesh and Vietnam, the UK is helping improve spending procedures, accounting and auditing. These changes help ensure money is spent for its intended purposes.

- Helping education, health and other ministries to recruit more staff, improve training, and use planning and monitoring to improve the way services are managed.

- Linking institutions between countries to share lessons and skills. UK organisations such as the police service and National Audit Office are working with sister organisations in poor countries. Exchanges between tax agencies within Africa are another example.

2.20 International partners can also help strengthen accountability by supporting 'watch-dog agencies', such as national auditors, anti-corruption commissions, ombudsmen and regulators, and human rights commissions. Providing more public information on local budgets in Uganda and India is reducing corruption by local government officials.[8] Independent customer surveys in Bangalore between 1994 and 2003 produced dramatic improvements in services such as water, policing, public transport and hospitals.

2.21 The media and civil society organisations hold governments to account. The media ask tough questions and encourage debate. Business associations pinpoint how to improve conditions for investment and remove red tape. Civil society groups such as trade unions, co-operatives and faith groups press for better public services. In many countries, civil society is helping to improve the quality of public spending by identifying whether the poor – including women and disabled people – will benefit. In Bolivia, they are monitoring the use of oil revenues. In Bangladesh, grassroots organisations are helping members get land rights. The UK will do more to support such work.

2.22 In many societies, women have less power over their lives than men. Reducing poverty means helping them get their rights, helping them hold officials to account and enabling them to engage in the political process. The UK is committed to promoting women's and girls' rights, particularly through partnerships between civil society organisations and governments.

Helping change in Iraq

In the south of Iraq, the UK is working with the BBC World Service Trust. We have provided training for Iraqi journalists, and established an independent Iraqi-run TV and radio broadcast station which went on air in summer 2005. Programmes include debates between election candidates, face-to-face interviews with senior politicians and phone-in discussions. These broadcasts help hold local and national government to account. For example, in a past programme a provincial governor faced hard-hitting questions about how local government funds were being used.

2.23 International links between civil society groups – such as those promoted by UK trade unions, the Commonwealth Secretariat, and the British Council – can help improve governance and accountability. We will provide more support for such initiatives in future.

The UK will

- Set up a new £100 million Governance and Transparency Fund to strengthen civil society and the media to help citizens hold their governments to account.

- Work in our partner countries to help make public institutions more accountable, for example by strengthening parliamentary and regulatory oversight.

- Support public sector reform to help improve public services.

- Support more responsive governance, for example, by helping partner countries to consult with poor people, and to produce better statistics on poverty and monitor their progress in overcoming it.

- Improve the effectiveness of our technical assistance, pool our funding with other donors where possible, increase the use of local providers and ensure value for money.

- Implement an Africa Capacity Building Initiative to share knowledge and skills between UK central and local government and developing countries.

Winning the fight against corruption…

2.24 Corruption hurts poor people, and it harms women in particular.[9] When health staff demand bribes for medicines, teachers for enrolling children in school, or local government officials for providing water connections, it keeps people poor. Corruption damages economic growth by increasing the cost of doing business. It siphons off resources that should go into public services. And it undermines the accountability of political leaders and officials to their citizens. When politicians are 'bought' by powerful people or businesses through bribery, or when leaders themselves use personal or public funds to buy support, they become representatives of the few and not the many. In short, corruption is both a cause and a symptom of bad governance.

2.25 Reducing red tape and simplifying procedures limits opportunities for extortion. Improving pay and conditions helps reduce the incentives for officials to take bribes in the first place. Making tax collection agencies independent of other government institutions raises standards and performance. Automating financial systems and improving public contracting practices further reduces the scope for corruption. And appointing and managing people on merit leads to more professional and less corrupt public services. The UK will support these sorts of measures in countries where we provide aid.

2.26 But as well as more effective institutions, there is also a need for better accountability. Audit institutions, anti-corruption commissions and parliamentary committees need to scrutinise how government works. There must be proper laws and rules against corruption. Most countries have them, but they are completely ineffective if the police and legal system fail to investigate and prosecute offenders.

2.27 Popular political pressure also reduces the scope for corruption. A good example is the anti-corruption work of Transparency International (supported by the UK) in countries such as Kenya, Ghana, Zambia, Pakistan, and Bangladesh. Grassroots organisations and the media play a vital role in generating public debate about corruption by campaigning against it. Newspapers and radio stations have led the demand for action in high profile corruption cases in countries such as India, Kenya and Zambia.

2.28 The fight against corruption can be won, and public financial reforms are making a difference. A recent assessment of 26 Heavily Indebted Poor Countries shows that improvements are possible. For example, twice as many countries now produce expenditure reports showing how they are using their resources which reduces the risk of funds being misused.[10] And the UK is working with the World Bank, the European Commission (EC) and others to support a new international Public Expenditure Financial Accountability Framework which is putting pressure on governments to raise standards. The Framework has been used in nineteen countries and plans are in place to use it in a further 30.

Counting on education

At the African Inland Church Girls Primary School, like many others in Kenya, it isn't unusual to see the entire school budget written up on charts around the school. "This means," explains Deputy Headteacher Francisca Sanare, "that parents and the local community know exactly how much should be spent on the education of their children". The system allows parents to hold staff to account and helps prevent small scale corruption by ensuring that every available penny goes on the children's education. "Since we have had this system in place, parents have taken a keener interest in the running of the school and know exactly what each child is supposed to get. Even the children know that the government is providing them with pens, pencils and textbooks."

2.29 Tackling corruption is a long-term challenge and the UK's approach is four-fold. First, we will take all necessary steps to ensure that UK aid is used for the purpose intended. Strict accounting, procurement and auditing procedures are required for all UK aid programmes. Where necessary, independent auditors track expenditure, and technical staff strengthen management arrangements and oversight. All allegations of corruption are investigated and, if necessary, corrective action taken.

2.30 Second, the UK will help governments to investigate and deal with alleged corruption through the courts – especially where money has flowed through UK jurisdictions. The UK Serious Fraud Office has provided legal assistance to court cases in a large number of countries including Zambia, Malawi and Sierra Leone. The UK also uses its influence to support and encourage political leaders to take action, as recent events in Kenya and Nigeria have shown.

2.31 Third, corruption will be a central part of our discussions with partner governments when agreeing and reviewing our Country Assistance Plans. We will always assess our partners' commitment and actions to reduce corruption when deciding how to provide aid and what safeguards are required. We will now regularly review the 'quality of governance' as outlined above.

2.32 And fourth, in order to reduce the scope for international bribery and money laundering and to promote better codes of conduct for international businesses and public contracting, we will take action to address the international incentives for bad governance as set out in the next chapter.

Is Nigeria turning the corner on corruption?

Nigeria was bottom of the Transparency International Corruption Perceptions Index before 2000. But with strong political leadership and help from its international partners, the country is beginning to inch its way up the league. President Obasanjo and Finance Minister Okonjo-Iweala have set up agencies to investigate and prosecute corruption and – as several high profile individuals have found – corruption and financial crime now carry a real risk of prosecution. Revenue allocations to the country's 36 states and 774 local governments have been made public since 2004, so people can now see how much money their government has to spend. The National Assembly is considering new laws to strengthen budget controls and public contracting. The EITI in Nigeria is helping track the production of oil and gas and the public revenues it generates. Challenges remain, however, particularly in making information on government spending more widely available – but progress is being made.

The UK will

- Work with the World Bank and others to develop a new, internationally agreed approach to assessing and tackling corruption in all developing countries.

- Provide practical support to governments to help them investigate corruption, and deal with alleged offenders through the courts.

- Raise the issue of corruption with partner governments as part of our regular discussions.

- Help developing countries strengthen their public financial management, and support other public sector reforms to tackle corruption.

- Support the implementation of the Public Expenditure Financial Accountability Framework in order to increase international assistance to strengthen public finances in developing countries.

- Support independent organisations (watch-dogs, lobby groups etc) that monitor and track the performance of public services and organisations.

- Continue to investigate all allegations of corruption affecting UK aid, and take action.

How change happens: Enforcing land rights in Tajikistan

For poor people around the world, getting access to courts and legal support to protect their rights is often impossible. In many cases, the reason for this is straightforward – they cannot afford to pay the legal fees.

In Tajikistan, the UK has been helping to solve this problem by supporting Third Party Arbitration Courts. These courts are an alternative way of resolving disputes: two sides to a dispute agree to nominate a third party who they both trust to mediate their disagreement and come to a decision. Although they operate independently of the formal legal system, decisions are recognised by Tajikistan's official courts. This means that where parties do not comply with a decision voluntarily, the state can step in to enforce it.

Third Party Arbitration Courts provide poor people with a cheap, fair and accessible way of resolving disputes and protecting their rights. They are particularly effective at protecting the rights of women to land and property.

UK support to Third Party Arbitration Courts has helped to make legal services available to 800,000 people in Tajikistan (12% of the population). The approach has also been used successfully in Russia, Kyrgyzstan, Moldova, Ukraine and Georgia.

chapter 3
supporting good governance internationally

> Incentives for good governance are heavily influenced by the international economy, the behaviour of other governments and the private sector.
>
> International co-operation is essential to tackle bribery, corruption and money laundering.
>
> Transparent management of government revenue and procurement is vital for good governance.

Governance is an international issue…

3.1 The global economy offers great opportunities for economic growth and development. Goods, money and people move around the world more than ever before. Transferring money has never been easier. But without suitable regulation, these opportunities can be abused. In too many cases, public money has been diverted for personal gain and the proceeds of bribery and corruption have been hidden away in financial centres around the world.

3.2 The Commission for Africa and the G8 at Gleneagles set out what the international community can do to prevent international corruption and crime and promote better use of resources. The UK is committed to taking these recommendations forward.

3.3 Chapter 2 set out what needs to be done in developing countries to build better governance. But, where governments do not or cannot regulate, international standards help to:

- Encourage responsible behaviour by companies.
- Tackle corruption by closing the international loopholes that allow people to get away with illicit gains.
- Promote better governance by helping build accountability within states.

Democratic Republic of Congo – the origins of bad governance

The Democratic Republic of Congo (DRC) was initially created as a commercial enterprise by King Leopold II of Belgium and subsequently governed to enable the ruling class to exploit its massive natural wealth. This was either used to buy off opponents or salted away overseas in personal bank accounts. Since the fall of Mobutu, work by organisations such as Global Witness shows that the government still does not ensure that DRC's natural resources are managed in the interests of the people.[1] Some of those in power bolster their positions through exploitation of natural resources in partnership with unscrupulous international investors, sometimes supported by foreign governments. In 2004, government revenue from the mining sector was only US$15 million. It is estimated that the state lost revenues ten times this amount, money that could have been invested in providing health care and education.

International standards encourage responsible behaviour…

3.4 Governments need to be able to stop unscrupulous individuals or companies profiting from activities such as paying bribes, illegal trading in natural resources or selling arms that fuel conflict.

3.5 The best solution is for the government of the country where such activity has taken place to have effective domestic legislation and regulation to stop it. However, where domestic capacity is weak, international codes of practice can encourage companies to work legitimately in developing countries. The OECD Guidelines for Multinational Enterprises, for example, set out what companies can do to meet standards on human rights, labour conditions, the environment and corruption. Some countries, including the UK, have found it difficult to respond to allegations of bad conduct under these Guidelines.[2] We are committed to following up specific cases more effectively in future.

3.6 Illegal trade in natural resources like diamonds or timber often pays for and prolongs conflict. In places like Sierra Leone and Liberia, the international community has set up expert monitoring panels to recommend sanctions, but has often been slow to act. Establishing standards on how to manage revenues from natural resources in conflict-affected countries would help address this problem. Stronger enforcement of UN sanctions – including better monitoring – would make international action quicker and more effective at cutting off the money that fuels conflict.

3.7 Export credit agencies are the largest source of public funds for private sector projects in the world. These agencies need to make sure that they are not supporting companies or their agents who may be paying bribes. The UK has recently strengthened the anti-bribery procedures of its Export Credits Guarantee Department. But, because export credit agencies are in competition with each other, their standards and behaviour need to be agreed at an international level.

3.8 Developing countries, like all states, have the right to acquire the means to protect themselves – which means buying arms. But many arms that find their way into conflicts – for example in Somalia – are arranged by unscrupulous brokers exploiting loopholes in national legislation or breaking

Natural resources are in conflict zones

Source: Adapted from Philippe Rakacewicz, in Atlas du Monde diplomatique 2003, Paris www.mondediplo.com

arms embargoes. The UK Government is committed to making sure that exporters licensed by us do not contribute to conflict or human rights abuses.

3.9 There is currently no international agreement to regulate the trade in conventional weapons. That is why the UK wants an international, legally binding Arms Trade Treaty that will increase transparency and prevent arms transfers that make conflicts worse. Negotiating such a treaty would give developing countries a say in creating a system which would benefit all countries.

Too many guns

"There is lack of security here," says Elona Krasniçi, a woman from Shkodër, Albania. "No parent is calm about their children going to school... because everyone possesses a gun – without permission in most cases. We can see these people possessing guns in everyday life, we hear it in the news – this person was killed, this other killed himself. So all of this information creates an overall sense of the lack of security in the family, society and everywhere else."

Source: Saferworld

The UK will

- Launch a revamped National Contact Point by September 2006 with the involvement of DFID, the Foreign and Commonwealth Office (FCO) and independent experts as well as the Department for Trade and Industry to strengthen our implementation of the OECD Guidelines for Multinational Enterprises.

- Work within the OECD to make the Guidelines more effective in promoting responsible business conduct, particularly in countries with weak governance.

- Press the international community to tackle the trade in conflict resources; promote international standards on the management of natural resource revenues in countries affected by or at risk of conflict; help set up an international expert panel in the UN to monitor the links between natural resources and conflict; and support improvements in the monitoring of UN sanctions.

- Work with governments and civil society to secure agreement at the UN General Assembly in 2006 to start talks on an Arms Trade Treaty that is legally binding, covers all conventional weapons and the world's major arms exporters, includes enforcement and monitoring arrangements, and report progress to the UN General Assembly by 2008.

- Work with others to deal with the misuse and inappropriate export of small arms and light weapons.

- Ensure, when assessing export licences, that UK arms exports do not undermine development, for example by endangering human rights or increasing the risk of conflict.

- As part of the overall review of strategic arms export licensing laws in 2007, examine how well regulations to control the activities of arms brokers are working and whether these need to be changed or strengthened.

- Fully implement a new OECD 'action statement' on bribery that reduces the risk of export credit agencies providing financial support to companies that bribe overseas, and press other OECD countries to take similar action.

International standards help fight corruption…

3.10 The proceeds of corruption are often spent or saved outside the country. Some notorious leaders, like Presidents Mobutu of Zaire, Abacha of Nigeria and Marcos of the Philippines, looted spectacular amounts from their own countries. But huge amounts of money are now being returned to developing countries. Nigeria, for example, has received US$608 million from Switzerland and US$149 million from Jersey.[3]

3.11 The United Nations Convention Against Corruption (UNCAC) came into force in December 2005, and was ratified by the UK in February 2006. It is the first worldwide agreement on corruption. One hundred and forty countries have agreed to co-operate on all aspects of preventing, investigating and prosecuting corruption, returning stolen assets, and supporting each other on extraditions, investigations, prosecutions and judicial proceedings. The UN Office on Drugs and Crime has been asked to oversee and co-ordinate help for countries to put the UNCAC into practice.

3.12 The UK is committed to tackling corruption, bribery and money laundering. This includes making sure that we rigorously enforce relevant UK laws so that people who pay bribes are prosecuted, and assets are returned to the countries from which they have been stolen.

3.13 Following up allegations of bribery and money laundering is difficult if developing countries do not have the ability to produce evidence of sufficient quality to enable an international investigation. If developing countries request it, the UK will provide help – 'mutual legal assistance' – in tracking down laundered funds and gathering the evidence needed.

The other side of the coin[4]

In March 2006 the UK Africa All Party Parliamentary Group issued a report recommending how the UK could improve efforts to prevent and combat corruption in Africa. It also highlighted the UK's responsibility to help the three Crown Dependencies (Guernsey, Jersey and Isle of Man) and fourteen Overseas Territories (such as Bermuda, British Virgin Islands and Cayman Islands), many of which are important financial centres, to meet their international obligations. The report recommends: better co-ordination of the wide range of activities undertaken by different government departments and enforcement agencies; strengthening the ability of the UK and its Dependencies and Overseas Territories to return assets taken from developing countries; and working to reduce the risk of UK businesses being involved in bribery in developing countries. The Government will implement almost all of the report's recommendations.

3.14 Corruption and money laundering are frequently linked to other aspects of organised crime, such as illegal trafficking. Organised crime can corrupt political power and stifle the development of legitimate business. Vulnerable people are often the victims of illegal trade, whether it is drug smuggling or trafficking of human beings for sex. The UK is working to tackle organised crime from developing countries.

Human trafficking wrecks lives

Arta, 19, is from a small town in Serbia. A tough home life forced her to leave her home town in search of work. But things didn't turn out well. Her new boss sexually harassed her, and she was poorly paid. Arta decided to accept a job as a sex worker in Italy. The man who had offered her the job provided her with a false passport and transportation. As soon as she arrived, he took away all her documents. Arta was forced to work as a prostitute in an area well known for its Serbian, Albanian and Russian mafia links. When she refused, she was beaten and raped. Ten days later a client helped her to escape.

Source: Astra (Serbian NGO)

The UK will

- Publish an annual UK Action Plan to tackle corruption affecting developing countries, particularly in Africa. The International Development Secretary will oversee and report progress against this every six months.

- Set up a dedicated overseas corruption unit by the end of 2006, staffed by City of London and Metropolitan police with support from DFID and others, to investigate allegations of bribery and money laundering.

- Press our G8 partners to ratify the UNCAC by March 2007, and work with the UN Office on Drugs and Crime and other partners to ensure that it is implemented internationally.

- Make UK businesses aware of the risks of bribery overseas, and urge them to report instances of attempted bribery to UK embassies, so that they can be investigated by partner governments.

- Help developing countries in response to requests for Mutual Legal Assistance. This will include:

  - Deploying fast response teams from UK law enforcement and other organisations.
  - Supporting countries' ability to track assets and carry out investigations.
  - Drawing up proposals for an international corruption investigation centre which can provide professional help as part of implementing the UNCAC.

- Develop plans to tackle organised crime in a number of vulnerable developing countries.

- Help UK Overseas Territories and Crown Dependencies to put into practice relevant international agreements, such as the UNCAC and the OECD bribery convention, and measures equivalent to the EU directives on money laundering.

International standards promote better governance…

3.15 The international community must also help by agreeing standards of conduct which strengthen accountability and governance. For example, natural resources create wealth and jobs, but when they are mismanaged they can become a curse. Through the Extractive Industries Transparency Initiative (EITI), launched in 2002, governments make public the payments they receive from oil, gas and mining companies, and companies make public the payments they make to governments. This helps people to see how resources are being used, and to check there is no corruption.

3.16 Four years on, EITI is working successfully in countries like Nigeria and Azerbaijan. We will encourage more countries to join the Initiative, and will work to strengthen its implementation. The UK will push for a UN General Assembly resolution to establish the Initiative as an international standard of good practice. We will also discuss with others how the Initiative could be extended, for example, by covering revenue paid to local authorities, and revenue from pipeline usage.

3.17 Other natural resources, particularly forestry and fisheries, are also major sources of income for many poor countries. Initiatives like the Forest Law Enforcement, Governance and Trade partnerships and the High Seas Task Force on illegal, unregulated and unreported fishing are already trying to ensure that these resources are well managed. Just as EITI has succeeded by bringing together governments, companies and civil society, the UK will support these initiatives to ensure that revenues and exploitation rights are publicly scrutinised.

Fuelling accountability in Azerbaijan

Azerbaijan's future depends on its oil and gas resources, which are being developed by international companies. Azerbaijan joined the Extractive Industries Transparency Initiative in June 2003, as one of the first pilot countries. A National Committee on EITI was established in November 2003. Three EITI reports, published between March 2005 and January 2006, have sparked wide debate – especially where there are discrepancies between the numbers reported by companies and the Government. Azeri civil society is now better able to scrutinise the oil and gas sector and is more closely involved in discussions with the Government and the oil companies. In turn, this has stimulated a wider public debate on how transparency and accountability can contribute to democracy and the rule of law.

3.18 Public procurement is also a source of corruption. Transparency International's bribe payers' index suggests that the construction, defence, and health sectors are highly prone to bribery.[5] Using EITI-type principles to strengthen procurement in these areas will help governments manage their finances better. The UK will work with others to take this forward.

The UK will

- Sponsor a UN General Assembly resolution for EITI to become an international standard of good management; work closely with China, Russia and others to promote EITI; work with others to identify a permanent international secretariat for EITI; and develop a means of verifying whether countries and companies are doing what they promised. We will also propose that EITI is extended to other areas of revenue and spending in the oil, gas and mining sectors.

- Work with partners to develop codes of practice to make it easier to scrutinise forestry and fishery agreements and revenues, building on existing initiatives such as the EU Forest Law Enforcement, Governance and Trade partnerships and the High Seas Task Force.

- Build on the experience of EITI to help developing countries improve transparency and value for money in public procurement, and develop international proposals to increase scrutiny of public spending in the defence, construction and health sectors to help fight corruption.

How change happens: Stopping the trade in 'blood' diamonds

Diamond mining could help reduce poverty in many developing countries. But stones from diamond-rich countries like Sierra Leone, DRC, Liberia and Angola among others have instead fuelled conflicts and corruption. These stones are often called 'blood' or 'conflict' diamonds.

The Kimberley Process, set up in 2003, is a certification system designed to record the origin of rough diamonds and assure buyers that a particular stone originates from a legitimate source. It now covers the vast majority of international trade in rough diamonds. It has helped to reduce significantly the flows of illicit diamonds and to end trade with countries accused of involvement with them.

As a result, the Kimberley Process has cut the chances of conflict diamonds helping illegitimate governments, warlords and rebels to buy guns and launder money. It has also led to substantial increases in the proportion of rough diamonds exported through official channels – which boosts government revenues that can then be used to fight poverty. The value of official diamond exports from the DRC rose from US$642 million in 2003 to US$720 million in 2004 and US$431 million in the first half of 2005 alone. It is estimated that 80% of diamonds produced in Sierra Leone are now sold on the legitimate market.

But despite this impressive progress, conflict diamonds still exist. More needs to be done to ensure that the Kimberley Process captures all diamond trading, and to strengthen government controls along the whole supply chain.

helping people get security, incomes, and public services

chapter 4
promoting peace and security

> **Security is a precondition for development.**
>
> **Preventing conflict is better than trying to pick up the pieces afterwards.**
>
> **The international community has a 'responsibility to protect' when states fail to protect their civilians from genocide, war crimes and crimes against humanity.**

Insecurity and conflict keep people poor...

4.1 Poor people want to feel safe and secure just as much as they need food to eat, clean water to drink and a job to give them an income. Without security there cannot be development. Farmers cannot farm if they are afraid that their land, livestock or family will be attacked. Girls cannot be educated if they are scared of the journey to school. And businesses will not invest where there is fighting, or where the rule of law is not upheld.

4.2 The number of armed conflicts around the world has dropped by 40% since the early 1990s. Even in Africa there has been a decrease in recent years.[1] The international community, including the UK, has helped prevent conflict and build peace. However, there is still a lot of violence and new pressures threaten to cause further instability in developing countries – especially increasing competition over natural resources and, in Asia, rising inequality.

4.3 War and insecurity have a devastating impact. Of the 34 countries furthest from reaching the MDGs, 22 are in, or just coming out of, conflict.[2] In Africa, there are more than 12 million internally displaced people as a result of violence.[3] Violent conflict reverses economic growth, causes hunger, destroys roads, schools and clinics, and forces people to flee across borders. Most of the 3.9 million people that have died in the DRC's conflict, died of disease.[4] Women and girls are particularly vulnerable because they suffer sexual violence and exploitation. And violent conflict and insecurity can spill over into neighbouring countries and provide cover for terrorists or organised criminal groups.[5]

A victim of violence

After being abducted at the age of ten, Francis Owot spent almost ten years fighting as a child soldier in the bush in northern Uganda. "After I was abducted, we moved the whole day until night. We woke up in the morning, we started marching, then after two weeks, I saw that there is no change. I sat under a tree crying, when they got me I was beaten. I was still a child, still young, but they were teaching me the use of a gun." Francis eventually became a willing fighter. "Fighting," he says, "was part of my work. And if I stayed for two weeks without firing, I would feel something was missing, something is not very normal." Francis escaped from the bush and now lives in a refugee camp with his family.

Source: Mergelsberg, B. (2005) Crossing Boundaries: Experiences of Returning "Child Soldiers"

Has the number of armed conflicts gone up or down in the last 60 years?[6]

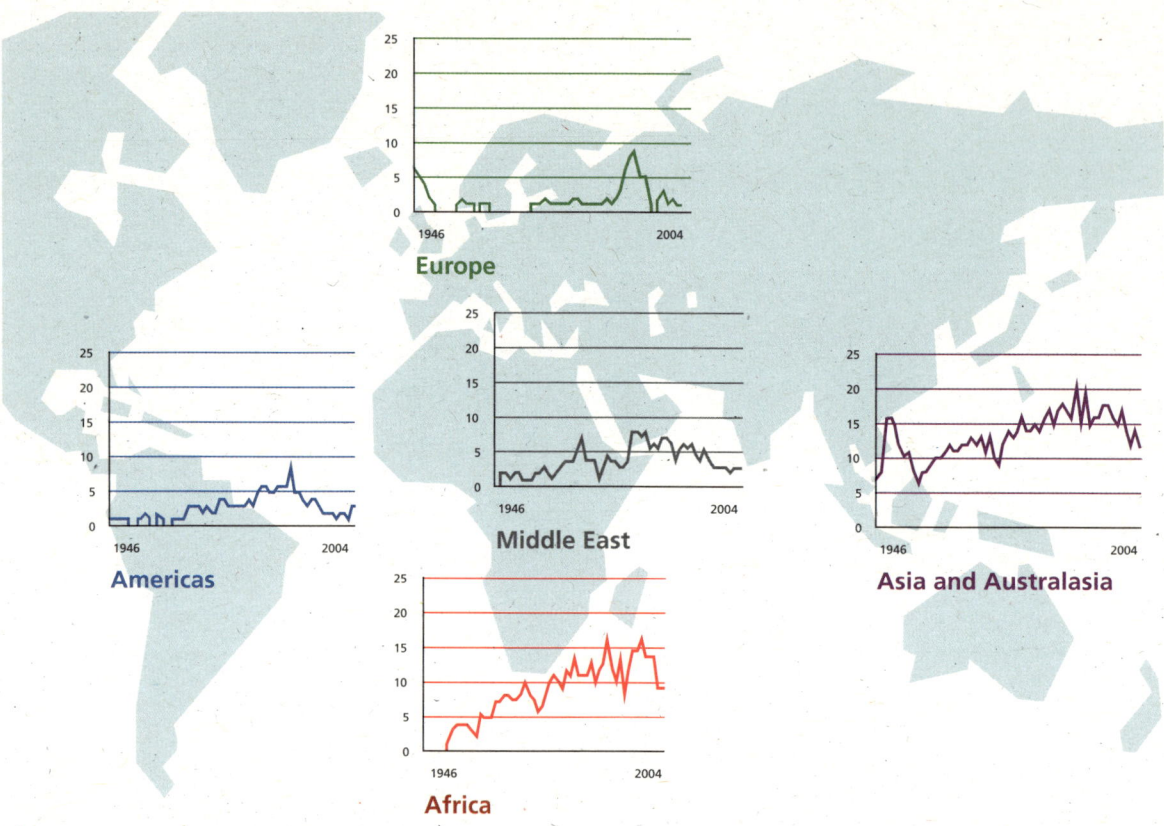

Source: PRIO/Uppsala Armed Conflict Dataset, as described in Gleditsch et al. (2002) and updated in Harbom & Wallensteen (2005) Journal of Peace Research.

4.4 At the G8 Gleneagles meeting and the UN World Summit in 2005, the international community agreed that more needed to be done to prevent conflict. Development, diplomatic and security efforts must complement each other better to achieve this. We believe there are two big challenges:

- First, helping developing countries to build effective and accountable institutions to provide security and justice to the poor.

- Second, ensuring that the international community builds capacity to prevent and deal with conflict.

Improving security and preventing conflict…

4.5 People need effective states to provide them with security. This means protecting citizens and dealing justly with those who commit crime. It means managing the causes of insecurity and conflict from both within and outside their borders. This requires effective institutions – police, military, border controls, and a legal and judicial system – that are overseen by civilian authorities.

4.6 Weak or corrupt governments are often responsible for some of the worst human rights abuses. In Burma and Zimbabwe violence has been sponsored by the state. Poor governance breeds disillusionment, grievances and conflict. People who live with constant abuse of power, or who cannot get justice or express their views peacefully, are more likely to turn to violence. While there is no evidence that poverty contributes directly to terrorism, or that terrorists come from poorer communities, they often justify their actions by claiming to be fighting against injustice. They exploit poverty and exclusion in order to tap into popular discontent – taking advantage of fragile states such as Somalia, or undemocratic regimes such as in Afghanistan in the 1990s, to plan violence.

4.7 Countries with good governance are less likely to face these problems. Fighting poverty and social exclusion through better governance therefore contributes to security – locally and internationally – and helps to reduce the potential for radicalisation or extreme political violence.

4.8 International partners can help developing countries to improve security by getting arms out of circulation, reforming police and armed forces, improving courts and prisons, and giving people economic and political alternatives to violence and extremism. The UK supports such work through our aid programme and our conflict prevention pools (see below). But this is not just about aid. As we set out in the previous chapter, international partners must also help improve security by tackling the trade in arms and reducing the risk of international corruption.

4.9 Helping countries to prevent war is far more cost-effective than helping them rebuild afterwards.[7] Having neglected Afghanistan during the 1990s, the international community will need to spend US$20 billion to help reconstruct the country.[8] But to prevent conflict, international partners must first understand the causes of conflict and ensure their aid does not unintentionally fuel it. After

analysing the conflict in Nepal, the UK changed the focus of our aid programme to ensure that previously excluded social groups and regions were able to access public services.

4.10 Early analysis of the causes of conflict or instability also helps the international community to anticipate potential crises. The EU and African Union (AU) have 'early warning' systems and the UN monitors the risk of humanitarian crises through its Office for the Co-ordination of Humanitarian Affairs. However, none of these mechanisms will be effective until there are better international arrangements to turn early warning into early action. Without a stronger commitment to act, and the capacity to do so, the international community's response to conflict will continue to be inconsistent and inadequate.

Better security, better development

In Malawi the UK has helped tackle failings in the criminal justice system by introducing a paralegal advisory service for vulnerable people, training traditional rulers to improve local dispute resolution, and providing victim support units for women and children in district police stations.

In Jamaica, DFID, the Home Office the FCO and other UK agencies are working together to help the government tackle armed violence in poor urban communities.

In Afghanistan, the UK is supporting efforts to reduce the supply of opium through better law enforcement and by providing opportunities for poor farmers and labourers to develop alternative, legal livelihoods. And in Helmand province, DFID is investing in small community projects in unstable areas to improve security and encourage development.

The UK will

- Work with developing countries and other international partners to improve security and access to justice for the poor.
- Through our aid programme and the UK conflict prevention pools, increase our investment in at least ten countries where security has been identified as a priority by:
  - Undertaking more work on safety, security and access to justice.
  - Supporting security sector reform.
  - Reducing the proliferation of small arms and light weapons.
  - Supporting disarmament, demobilisation and reintegration programmes for ex-combatants.
  - Supporting initiatives to tackle social exclusion and radicalisation.
- Assess the causes of conflict and insecurity as part of our new governance assessment and use this to shape UK development policy and programmes.

Tackling conflict and building peace…

4.11 For people living in constant fear of violence, as in Darfur, Northern Uganda and (in the past) Rwanda, the ultimate test of the international community – and particularly the UN – is the willingness to take action to protect civilians when states fail in their responsibilities.

4.12 At the UN World Summit, all 191 UN Member States endorsed for the first time the groundbreaking principle of a 'responsibility to protect'. They agreed that while individual governments are responsible for the protection of their own people, the international community would no longer tolerate inaction by national governments in the face of genocide, war crimes, ethnic cleansing and crimes against humanity within their borders. Translating this commitment into action means using diplomacy, humanitarian assistance and sanctions to protect civilians; and as a last resort, collective military action authorised by the UN Security Council.

4.13 When states fail or cannot govern, the UN has unique authority to speak out and step in. It represents the will of the whole international community. But other international and regional organisations including the EU, the AU, the North Atlantic Treaty Organisation (NATO), the Organisation for Security and Co-operation in Europe, and sub-regional groups like the Economic Community of West African States (ECOWAS) also have important roles to play in preventing and managing conflict. These organisations need stronger capacity, and, in the case of the UN, major reform. They also need clearer arrangements for working together.

4.14 Mediation through the UN, AU and sub-regional bodies is critical to resolving conflict. More civil wars have been brought to an end in the past fifteen years through negotiation than in the previous two centuries.[9] Diplomatic efforts by the UK and other international partners can help – as we are trying to do in Darfur. And, behind the scenes, local and non-governmental organisations play an important role in defusing conflict and reconciling communities. Mediation efforts deserve more international support.

Mediating crises

Regional mediation for peace in Sudan: The Comprehensive Peace Agreement between North and South Sudan in January 2005 ended a twenty year war that killed an estimated 2 million people. A team drawn from the governments of the region worked with the chief mediators from the North and South, facilitating negotiations on contentious issues, often for weeks at a time.[10] The UK, Norway and the US underpinned these efforts by providing financial support, expert input for the mediation process, and diplomatic and political assistance.

Grass roots mediation in Somalia: The "Somali Dialogue for Peace" Project, helped ensure a peaceful parliamentary election process in Somaliland in 2005 by developing codes of conduct for the political parties and media, and by facilitating dialogue to avoid violence in the territories disputed between Somaliland and Puntland.[11] The project has also worked to address long-standing clan conflict that has obstructed humanitarian and development work in Mudug and Galgadud in the central regions of Somalia.

4.15 But the international community must also be ready to act to protect civilians where necessary. The demand for peace support operations is increasing. There are currently nineteen UN peace support operations underway around the world employing 62,000 troops, 6,000 police and 15,700 civilians.[12] At present the UK has 300 armed forces personnel in UN peace support operations. We provide training to countries who contribute troops to the UN and are helping to make the UN's Department of Peacekeeping Operations more effective. But the UN's planning ability along with the availability of peacekeepers, police, transport, medical and engineering facilities are stretched to the limit. Much greater international investment is needed to build capacity for peace support operations. As well as the UN, this should cover other regional organisations like the AU. The EU and NATO can play a particularly important role in providing high quality forces able to respond quickly to new crises. And, alongside peacekeeping, other measures are needed to protect people such as using human rights monitors and encouraging the media to report what is going on.

4.16 Countries have a 44% risk of falling back into conflict in the first five years after the end of a civil war.[13] The UN Peacebuilding Commission has been set up to change this by ensuring that post-conflict countries get long term help. Important lessons have been learnt from the Democratic Republic of Congo and Afghanistan. There has to be a shared plan between the government and international partners that focuses on security, the rule of law and development. Achieving rapid, visible improvements that maintain public support for peace is vital. Funds should be pooled to reduce the burden on weak governments. And funding should be provided throughout the reconstruction phase, not just in the immediate period after the conflict. The Peacebuilding Commission will need to act on these lessons and improve co-ordination between national governments and their international partners, including the UN, World Bank and IMF.

Working across government to stop conflict

The Global Conflict Prevention Pool (GCPP) and the Africa Conflict Prevention Pool (ACPP) were jointly established in 2001 by DFID, FCO and MOD to improve the UK's work in conflict prevention, conflict management and peacebuilding. GCPP funding has helped the UN Office for the High Commissioner for Human Rights in Nepal to monitor human rights and is supporting regional police training in Afghanistan. The ACPP has provided support for ECOWAS rapid response missions to Liberia and Cote d'Ivoire, paving the way for UN peace support operations, and significant support to ceasefire monitoring missions in Sudan. We will review the GCPP and the ACPP to ensure that they are as effective as possible.

The Post Conflict Reconstruction Unit, set up in 2004, enables UK Government Departments and the military to work together to support countries emerging from conflict. The Unit provides skilled civilian staff at short notice to help kick-start post-conflict recovery. It has helped plan for the UK military deployment to Helmand in Afghanistan and is supporting provincial reconstruction work in southern Iraq. We will continue to work through the Post Conflict Reconstruction Unit, including in Africa, where needed.

The UK will

- Work with others to ensure that the international agreement on 'responsibility to protect' is turned into a willingness to act in specific cases.

- Invest in monitoring human rights and support the media to raise awareness and gather evidence when states fail in their responsibilities.

- Work with others to ensure that the UN, AU, EU and other regional organisations have adequate capacity to prevent and respond to conflict by:
  - Monitoring countries that are vulnerable to conflict through effective early warning systems.
  - Mediating between conflicting groups, for example through the UN Secretary General's Special Representatives or the AU's Peace and Security Council and Panel of the Wise.
  - Responding when states are unable to protect their citizens.

- Press for better co-ordination between the UN and other international organisations involved in peacekeeping such as the AU, EU and NATO.

- Continue to push for a significant increase in the number of high-quality peacekeepers internationally, and train 75,000 troops by 2010 as agreed by the G8 in 2004 – including through the creation of an Africa Standby Force.

- Work to ensure that the EU and NATO develop effective rapid reaction forces able to respond quickly to crises, including in Africa, alongside the UN where appropriate.

- Contribute directly to UN mandated missions by providing UK troops and assets, subject to other commitments.

- Provide diplomatic and financial support to the new UN Peacebuilding Commission, the Peacebuilding Support Office and the Peacebuilding Fund.

- Through our development programmes and diplomatic efforts, ensure that the international response in post-conflict countries has strong national ownership, clear international leadership and pooled donor funding, and helps tackle poverty.

How change happens: Ending conflict in Sierra Leone

Sierra Leone has been devastated by civil conflict and is desperately poor. But, over the past few years, things have begun to change. The conflict is over, elections have been held and the new Government is committed to development and fighting corruption.

The UK played a major role in promoting peace, security and better governance in Sierra Leone. The UK military was sent in 2001-02 to support UN and ECOWAS peacekeepers and ensure elections could be held. The UK has helped the government to rebuild and train the new armed forces, reform the Ministry of Defence, reintegrate armed groups into society and overhaul the police service.

Since the conflict ended in 2002, the Government has begun to manage the economy more effectively, resulting in an annual GDP growth rate of 7.4%. Enrolment rates in primary schools have doubled since 2003. Child mortality rates are declining steadily and child immunisation rates have climbed from 28% in 1997 to 50% in 2004.

There is a long way to go, but the immediate danger of falling back into conflict is receding and the people of Sierra Leone now have hope for the future.

chapter 5
reducing poverty through economic growth

> Economic growth is the single most powerful way of pulling people out of poverty.
>
> Tackling inequality helps poor people participate in economic growth and trade.
>
> Reducing poverty sustainably means ensuring that today's development successes do not become tomorrow's environmental failures.

Growth is the best way to reduce poverty…

5.1 Poverty is about lack of opportunity, not just a lack of income. The lesson from the last 50 years is that economic growth is the most powerful way of pulling people out of poverty. Economic growth creates higher incomes, which help people save, invest and protect themselves when times are hard. Higher family incomes mean children can go to school rather than have to work. And as economies grow, governments can raise the money they need for public services.

5.2 Over recent decades, Asia has seen dramatic economic growth, first in the East Asian 'Tigers' of South Korea, Singapore and Taiwan, then Thailand, Malaysia and Indonesia, and more recently in China and Vietnam. Trade and openness to the international economy have been the key to this economic success. There has also been significant progress in South Asia. In the 1990s, economic growth helped reduce poverty in the region from just over 40% to around 30%.[1]

5.3 The picture is very different in sub-Saharan Africa, though there have been some success stories. Uganda and Ghana, for example, had high enough growth during the 1990s to reduce poverty by more than 10%. But the percentage of people living in poverty in the region as a whole has increased in the past two decades. There are now over 300 million poor people in sub-Saharan Africa.[2]

Struggling to grow in Malawi

Mary Banda lives on a small plot of land in rural Malawi. She plants maize at the start of the rainy season. Mary would like to buy new seeds and fertiliser but this is the time of year when she is shortest of cash. Even in good years she relies on food aid for the hungry months. In times of drought, or when there's an illness at home, the family have to sell their possessions and livestock just to survive. It takes years to regain them. Mary needs to find work or sell something to bring in cash but few local people have enough money to start a business, and the area has poor roads, electricity and phone connections. The nearest market is eight miles away and she cannot be sure that she will be able to sell or buy what she needs there.

Which regions have been getting richer?[3]

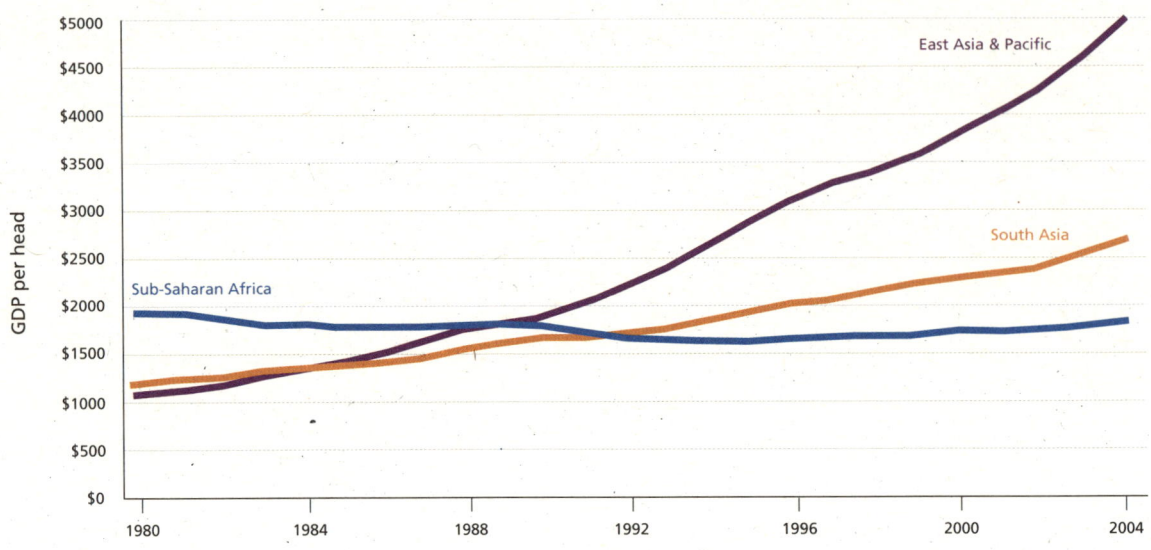

Source: World Development Indicators 2006

5.4 We believe there are five big challenges for the future:

- First, helping poor countries to grow faster, especially those lagging behind or who have the biggest numbers of poor people.

- Second, enabling poor men and women to benefit from growth, by providing better access to economic opportunities.

- Third, ensuring that growth is based on the sustainable use of natural resources, given rising worldwide consumption and the threat of climate change.

- Fourth, successfully negotiating for a fairer international trade system from which developing countries can benefit.

- Fifth, managing migration to promote growth.

Promoting growth…

5.5 It is the private sector – from farmers and street traders to foreign investors – that creates growth. Growth is fuelled by the creativity and hard work of entrepreneurs and workers. But as the Commission for Africa emphasised, it is governments that are in a position to make markets and competition work, by taking the lead in making business easier and less expensive, and determining the level of regulation.

5.6 Some developing countries are hardly growing at all. This is often because the government is not managing the economy well. High and unstable inflation makes business difficult. And local and foreign investors take fewer risks if corruption means they have to pay bribes for licences, or if legal systems fail to uphold contracts. Growth happens faster when political and economic leaders create the right environment for trade and investment.

How did Botswana grow?

From 1965 to 1998 Botswana's economy grew at an annual rate of 7.7%. External threats during the 19th century helped unite tribal and ethnic groups. This contributed to a common interest in building a strong state following independence in 1966 to safeguard property rights, improve infrastructure, and keep up the traditional 'kgotla' or public meeting so that government listened to the needs of the community. It created the stability and confidence necessary for investment and led to policies that benefited the whole country – so that Botswana's huge mineral revenue was used to boost national development, rather than being siphoned off for the benefit of a small elite.

5.7 One of the lessons of recent decades is that there is no single path to growth. Some of the reforms that international partners pushed through during the 1980s and 1990s did not work. However, while successful countries have followed a number of different policies to suit their own circumstances, they have based these reforms on common principles.

5.8 First, governments must establish macro-economic stability. This means that central banks and finance ministries must keep public borrowing and inflation at manageable levels, interest rates affordable and exchange rates stable and realistic. This makes costs and profits for businesses more predictable, which encourages investment. A strong financial sector also helps people to invest their savings and use resources effectively.

5.9 Second, governments need to remove unnecessary barriers to business, including obstacles to foreign trade and investment. Regulation is needed to make sure that workers earn a decent wage and have safe working conditions. But this should not make it too hard or expensive for people to set up in business. While some governments regulate too little, many regulate badly or too much, placing huge costs on the private sector. For example, it takes two procedures and two days to start a business in Australia, but fourteen procedures and 153 days in Mozambique. In Singapore, it takes seven hours and two signatures to clear goods through customs but in Bangladesh, it takes seven days and 38 signatures.[4] Improved business conditions in China and India during the 1980s and 1990s meant that private investment nearly doubled. Countries which improve their regulation to the best international standards can increase growth by as much as 2.3% a year.[5]

Changing the climate for business

The Investment Climate Facility (ICF), launched in June 2006, aims to boost growth in Africa by reducing barriers to private sector investment. It will create more and better jobs, particularly in small-scale businesses and will help:

- Improve the image of Africa as a place to do business.
- Improve business regulation, including fairer and more efficient taxation and customs.
- Strengthen property and contract rights.
- Develop Africa's financial markets, and investment in infrastructure.

The ICF will work with African governments, private-sector, regional and specialist organisations. The UK has played a leading role in helping to shape the ICF. We are contributing US$30 million over its first three years.

5.10 Third, investment in infrastructure is critical. Africa in particular suffers from a lack of energy, communications and irrigation. The costs of building, operating and maintaining infrastructure in developing countries are usually between 6% and 8% of gross domestic product (GDP), but investment can bring big returns.[6] Public-private partnerships – often supported by aid contracts or guarantees – can help. However, countries will need to adapt their infrastructure to deal with the risks posed by climate change.

Getting connected

"In the past, I had to carry rice on my shoulders to the Thua market, which is 7km away," says Kieu Van Do, a member of the Duong Quang commune in Vietnam. But the road running through the commune has recently been improved, and, like everyone, Kieu Van Do is delighted. Since the road improvement, incomes in the commune have increased annually by 7% and the commune has expanded into rearing livestock and selling services. At the same time schools, health clinics, power supplies and the post office have all been modernised.

Investing in infrastructure

The Commission for Africa argued for an extra US$10 billion a year in funding for infrastructure from 2005 to 2010, and US$20 billion in the following five years. International partners are on course to meet these targets. The Infrastructure Consortium for Africa was established by the G8 to increase investment in infrastructure. The UK provided initial finance of US$20 million to help establish the Consortium. In its first year, Consortium members secured funding for ten regional projects worth US$750 million, 34 country projects worth US$1.8 billion, and agreed scoping studies that will lead to further rounds of projects. Asia's infrastructure is better developed than Africa's but the total investment needed is higher. A new Asian Private Infrastructure Financing Facility is to be launched soon. International financial institutions like the World Bank and the Asian and African Development Banks are helping to bridge the funding gaps, improve procurement and technical standards, and stimulate private sector investment.

5.11 Fourth, agriculture is central to the economies of many poor countries and the lives of many poor people. Agriculture creates jobs and income, and helps the rest of the economy to grow by boosting demand for local goods and services. For every US$1 of farm income in Zambia, a further US$1.5 of income is generated in other businesses.[7] But to expand agriculture, governments need to guarantee land ownership, make sure that regulation, standards and subsidies are appropriate, and see that land is used sustainably so it continues to be productive. They also need to invest in infrastructure (for irrigation and to get goods to market) and innovation (including adaptation to climate change); and promote access to rural financial services. The G8 is supporting national and regional initiatives under the AU/NEPAD's Comprehensive African Agriculture Development Programme.

5.12 Growth is especially important in the wake of conflict and where the state is weak. The private sector in fragile states can create jobs and provide some services when governments are unable to. But re-establishing a favourable investment climate can be difficult. Getting the timing of reforms right and rebuilding basic infrastructure is essential. Sometimes, just getting the macro-economy under control can attract large-scale investment.

5.13 The UK believes that growth is the 'exit strategy' for aid. To reduce poverty quickly, international partners need to put growth at the heart of their relationships with developing countries. Multilateral and bilateral donors can support growth and macro-economic stability by providing advice and financial support to countries, and by co-operating closely with the international and local private sector.

CDC: Boosting the private sector

CDC Group plc (a company wholly-owned by DFID) invests in poor developing countries and aims to attract private capital by showing that such investments are worthwhile. It is proving a great success. CDC has mobilised about £360 million of private investment since 2003 and its portfolio has grown by 60% to £1.6 billion. Its investment in African telecoms highlights its success. CDC was the first institutional investor in Celtel which now has telephone operations in fourteen countries, covering 30% of Africa's population. It has transformed access to telephones for more than 5 million customers.

The UK will

- Support investment climate reforms, including through the Africa Investment Climate Facility, and help identify and address constraints to domestic and foreign investment.

- Increase investment in infrastructure by strengthening partner governments' capacity to prepare, finance, implement and maintain projects.

- Increase our support to private sector investment in infrastructure by at least £40 million over the next three years. With contributions from others, this will help double the amount of private sector investment to US$3 billion.

- Work with international partners to ensure that at least US$10 billion is provided annually for infrastructure in Africa by 2010 through the Africa Infrastructure Consortium.

- Work with multilateral development banks and development finance institutions such as the International Finance Corporation, the European Bank of Reconstruction and Development and the European Investment Bank to increase investment and support to the private sector, especially in difficult environments.

- Work closely with organisations like Business Action for Africa and the Commonwealth Business Council to identify ways to support development of the private sector and employment.

- As part of doubling research funding, we will increase support to science and technology to promote growth, including on agriculture, forestry and fisheries – for example through the AU/NEPAD's Comprehensive Agricultural Development Programme.

- Encourage developing country governments, the private sector and civil society, including trade unions, to work together to promote growth and employment.

Helping poor people to benefit from growth...

5.14 Inequality – the gap in incomes and opportunities between rich and poor – is a problem in many countries. It means that even if the economy is growing fast, the poor can still be left behind. Inequality causes social tensions, and unequal access to resources can mean that powerful vested interests continue to ignore the interests of the poor.

5.15 Growing now and redistributing the benefits later does not work.[8] Governments need to increase economic opportunities for all from the start. In Chapter 6 we set out how investment in education (especially for girls), health and social protection can boost opportunities and reduce the vulnerability that most poor people face. Investment in agriculture is especially important for many poor people. Investing in rural roads to link remote regions to local and regional markets, and providing access to new technology, like mobile phones, makes trade much easier. In most countries – as successful Bangladeshi NGOs have shown – more can also be done to help women fulfil their economic potential. Women must be able to borrow capital and access appropriate technology so that they can develop their businesses. Governments need to remove legislation that discriminates against women owning land or finding a job.

5.16 Access to finance helps poor people invest in productive assets like livestock, or goods for their business. Banks and governments need to work together to make credit more widely available. The UK contributes about £30 million a year to develop microfinance and financial services schemes – just one of these has attracted a further £58 million in private sector investment in the past five years.[9] Improved property rights are also important, as they provide collateral and encourage people to invest in the land. When rural households in Vietnam were given greater rights to farm land in 1988, it led to better and more productive land use, increased growth, and higher incomes.

5.17 Large numbers of poor people make their living as small traders and day labourers. Their ability to do this is greatly affected by local regulations like market licences and work permits. Small and medium sized enterprises account for about 40% of employment in low income African countries.[10] Governments need to help people in this sector to access business support services. As proposed by the Commission for Africa and NEPAD, an Africa Enterprise Challenge Fund is being set up to extend financial services, open markets to small producers and share skills between large and small companies.

Making markets work for poor people

Markets work for the poor when they provide opportunities for business and decent jobs, and enable poor people to get the goods and services they value. The UK is supporting a number of initiatives to expand such opportunities, including:

- In Southern Africa, the FinMark Trust is working with financial regulators, the banking sector and policy makers to extend access to financial services. In South Africa alone, the Trust's work has helped an additional 2.3 million people access financial services.

- In Bangladesh, the KATALYST programme is helping to strengthen business services for small and medium size enterprises. In Faridpur for example, KATALYST has been working with more than 3,000 fish farmers to increase the volume and quality of their production.

The UK will

- Help to tackle the barriers that prevent poor people from gaining access to markets and financial services, including by improving property rights.

- Support microfinance initiatives, particularly in partnership with banks and regulators.

- Promote good labour standards and work to get rid of child labour.

- Support the Africa Enterprise Challenge Fund with US$20 million in its first three years, and encourage others to provide a further US$40 million.

Using natural resources for sustainable growth…

5.18 A great deal of economic activity in developing countries depends on natural resources. Natural capital – which includes land, minerals, and forests – constitutes 5% of the world's wealth, but 26% of the wealth of developing countries (excluding oil-producing states).[11] But if exploitation of resources like oil, metals and timber is not regulated, or the resources are used inefficiently, it could undermine future growth. For example, Asia's rapid growth is, in some cases, being undermined by increasing consumption of natural resources and the costs and social inequities associated with it.[12] In Pakistan, build-up of salt in the soil, caused by overuse of irrigation, affects 16% of agricultural land, and contributes to the loss of over US$200 million a year in reduced crop yields.[13] And as we explore in Chapter 7, climate change will alter growing seasons and increase the risk of droughts and floods.[14]

5.19 Governments can do a number of things to make sure that natural resources are used sustainably and continue to help economies to grow. These include: removing inappropriate subsidies; regulating or taxing to discourage over-exploitation; clarifying exploitation rights; preventing illegal use; investing in innovation, such as better adapted crops and more efficient ways of using water and energy; and ensuring that these resources are priced properly. These challenges apply to developed and developing countries alike.

The UK will

- Help partner countries identify and respond to environmental opportunities and risks, for example by helping them to undertake strategic environmental assessments.

- With international partners, help countries to make efficient use of natural resources – especially water and energy.

- Reduce the impact of UK consumption, production and procurement on the global environment.

- Work with large developing countries through 'Sustainable Development Dialogues' to share experiences on managing the environmental impacts of growth.

Energy for growth

Economic growth is highly dependent on the availability and affordability of energy. Long term energy plans should aim at security, diversification and efficiency, and contain greenhouse gas emissions. For example, an energy strategy being developed by West African countries will help countries manage their energy resources, promote diversification and improve access to energy by poor people. In India, a long running programme in power sector reform, working in several Indian states, has reduced losses and improved public services and accountability.

Opening up trade…

5.20 International trade is vital for growth – as set out in the Government's 2004 White Paper on Trade and Investment.[15] It encourages competition and productivity, and helps developing countries earn their way out of poverty. But sub-Saharan Africa's share of world trade actually declined from 6% in 1980 to 2% in 2002.[16] Building trade with neighbouring countries is therefore especially important for Africa where intra-regional trade is only 5% of GDP, in contrast to East Asia and the Pacific where it is 27%.[17]

5.21 The best way of improving the access of developing countries to world markets is through a strong, multilateral rules-based trading system. The UK is working hard for an outcome to negotiations on the World Trade Organisation's Doha Development Agenda that leads to gains for all developing countries. This includes opening markets for goods like agricultural produce, industrial goods, textiles and clothing, substantially reducing all trade-distorting farm subsidies and ending export subsidies. But if it is to work, the World Trade Organisation agreement will have to meet the needs of countries at very different levels of development. Developing countries need

'special and differential treatment' in order, for instance, to protect vulnerable farmers from surges in food imports.

5.22 The EU has already made significant reforms to the Common Agricultural Policy. However, more radical reform will be needed, including during the 2008-09 review.[18] This should reduce agricultural subsidies which distort trade opportunities for developing countries and should encourage other OECD countries to phase out their agricultural subsidies. The EU's negotiation of Economic Partnership Agreements with African, Caribbean and Pacific countries offers another opportunity to increase trade. The UK is committed to ensuring that these agreements help reduce poverty.

A comparison of subsidies to agriculture and funding for development[19]

Aid for trade: helping generate growth

Aid for trade helps developing countries use opportunities for fairer and more open trade. The UK will increase our assistance to £100 million a year by 2010. Total donor commitments to date are about US$1 billion. Aid for trade could include customs reform, assistance to poor producers in meeting health and safety standards set by importing countries or supermarkets, and help with getting goods to market. For example, the UK is providing £4 million to help increase Southern Africa's exports of fruit, vegetables and other natural products by at least US$115 million by 2010. European and South African supermarkets will help small farmers find innovative ways to meet public and private product standards.

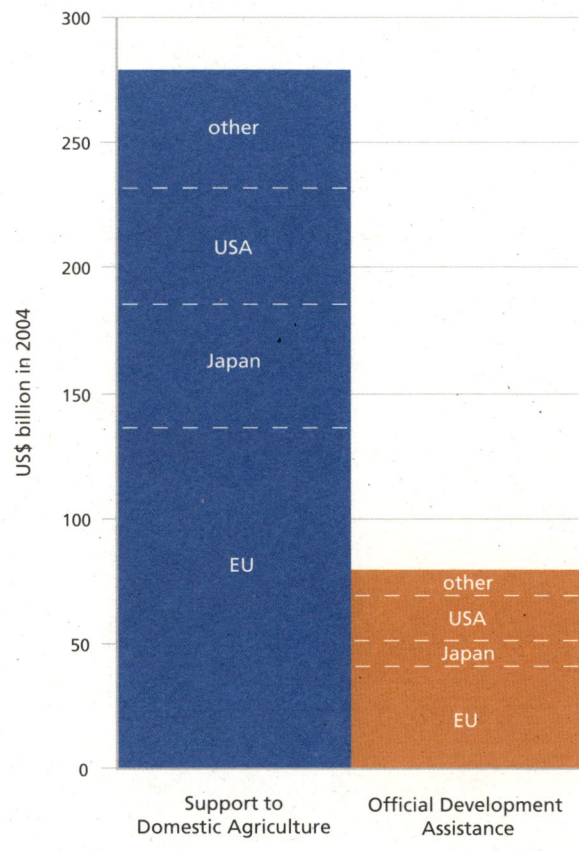

Source: OECD

5.23 While greater access to markets is vital, it is not enough by itself. To make the most of more open markets and regional trade, developing countries must be able to export the right goods at the right price. Developing countries need to build their ability to trade, and developed countries need to tackle the growing problem of non-tariff barriers. These include unreasonable product standards, or 'rules of origin' which prevent developing country businesses from buying raw materials from the most competitive sources.

The UK will

- Work with others to seek to ensure that the Doha Development Agenda delivers gains for developing countries, including significant market opening, reductions in trade-distorting farm support and the elimination of all forms of export subsidy by 2013.

- Work with EU partners to make sure that the 2008/09 review of the EU's Common Agricultural Policy leads to significant reform that benefits poor countries, and that EU Economic Partnership Agreements help African, Caribbean and Pacific countries increase economic growth and reduce poverty.

- Meet our pledge to increase our 'aid for trade' to £100 million a year by 2010 and encourage our G8 and EU partners to meet the commitments they made during our 2005 Presidencies.

Managing migration for growth...

5.24 For many families in poor countries, migration is an important way of earning a living. Between 50-80% of rural African households are said to have at least one migrant member in their own or a neighbouring country or further afield.[20] International migration has more than doubled in the past twenty years, with an estimated 200 million international migrants in 2005.[21]

5.25 Planning for and managing migration can help both to reduce poverty and meet the demand for labour in developed countries. It can also have a positive social and political impact as successful migrants return home. Money sent back by migrants plays an important part in sustaining the local economy. These 'remittances' through formal banking channels amounted to nearly US$167 billion in 2005 – much more than the combined aid rich countries gave in the same year.[22] In Lesotho, for example, remittances

account for 26% of the country's total national income.[23]

5.26 Developed countries can help poor people make the most of migration by: helping countries plan for and manage the consequences of it; understanding better the impact of their own immigration policies on development; supporting the efforts of migrant groups to help their home communities; and helping people to invest at home by making money transfers easier.

The UK will

- Work with partner countries and international organisations to seek ways in which both developing and developed countries can benefit from migration.

- Monitor the effect of our migration policy on development, including the points-based approach that the UK announced in March 2006.

- Work with the private sector and partners in the EU to make it easier for people to send remittances to help developing countries.

- Help partner governments to develop policies that help poor people to benefit from internal and international migration.

How change happens: Reducing poverty in Vietnam

In 1986 the Vietnamese Government approved a sweeping series of reforms known as doi moi to improve economic performance and combat poverty. Since then, Vietnam has made the transition from a centrally planned to a market-based economy. The result has been remarkable.

Since doi moi began, Vietnam has had one of the fastest growing economies in the world. Growth has averaged almost 7% over the entire period, and 7.6% for the last five years. Trade has driven much of this – exports increased by 19% a year during the 1990s. As a result, poverty has fallen at a breathtaking pace – from 65% in 1993 to 19% in 2004.

The Government has dedicated an increasing share of public expenditure to fight poverty and improve social welfare. Aid of over US$5 billion over the past ten years has financed about a third of total state investment. It has helped improve access to transport services, power, water and telephones, and is financing ambitious reforms, for example in banking and state-owned enterprises.

Aid also helped Vietnam to increase social sector spending fast and to reach its MDG targets early. Schooling in remote and poor regions has improved – reaching ethnic minority and other marginalised children. Access to safe water grew from 26% in 1993 to 49% in 2002, and electricity from 51% in 1996 to 88% in 2004. This has helped to underpin economic growth.

Of course, challenges remain. Corruption for one. Democratisation for another. But aid and growth are continuing to improve the lives of millions of people.

chapter 6
investing in people

Everyone should have access to health care, education, water and sanitation and, when times are hard, social security.

Real progress is possible, even in fragile states, but we all need to do a lot more.

Preventing the spread of HIV and treating people with AIDS is essential.

From commitments to results

6.1 All human beings have a right to food, clothing, shelter, education, health and social security. These are set out in the Universal Declaration of Human Rights and the Millennium Declaration.

6.2 Progress is possible. Since the 1960s, average life expectancy in developing countries has risen from 48 to 63 years.[1] In 1970 most adults in the world could not read or write, now most can. In sub-Saharan Africa and South Asia, adult literacy rates have doubled since 1970, and in East Asia they are now over 90%.[2] But progress is not fast enough. On current trends, most of the MDGs will be missed in sub-Saharan Africa and South Asia.

6.3 The UK believes there are four essential public services that are needed to make faster progress towards the MDGs: education, health, water and sanitation, and 'social protection' – various forms of direct help to poor families. In many developing countries these basic services are of poor quality and do not reach everyone.

6.4 Essential public services are linked to each other. When there is access to water, children can go to school rather than spend time fetching it. Going to school leads to better health. A girl who has been educated is much more likely to get her own children immunised, and healthy children are much less likely to drop out of school. Social protection helps children attend school or get to a health clinic. Investing in people – their skills, health and security – boosts economic growth and increases incomes. And having more money, in turn, gives people more choice, and generates the tax revenues which pay for public services.

6.5 We believe that there are four big challenges to providing essential public services:

- Developing country governments and the international community must spend more on public services.

- Developing countries will need to improve their capacity to provide more schools and clinics, and employ more teachers, doctors and nurses.

- Developing countries have to address the reasons why the poor – especially women, girls and disabled people – cannot access services.

- The international community will need to do more in fragile states, where there is the greatest risk that large numbers of poor people will be left behind.

6.6 In 2005, developing countries and the international community promised to tackle the first of these challenges by rapidly increasing financing for public services. Lack of funding has meant that many developing countries have been forced to limit what they want to do. In turn, international partners – some of whom were sceptical that increased resources would be used effectively – have focused on constraints rather than the scale of need. This cycle needs to be broken.

6.7 Developing countries now need to set out ambitious plans to reach the MDGs over the next ten years. And the international community must respond by funding these plans using the new aid they have promised. Where the circumstances are right, aid should be paid direct into government budgets. This aid needs to be long term and predictable, so that developing countries are able to make long term decisions to employ teachers and doctors, buy drugs, and build schools and clinics.

6.8 Second, as part of these plans, many developing countries will need to improve their capacity to provide good quality public services. Governments will need to strengthen and reform the organisations that provide education, health, water and social protection. They will also need better national and local monitoring to improve management of services and results.

6.9 Third, governments and partners have to address the problems which prevent poor people – especially women and children – from using services, even when they are available. This means doing something about user fees and discrimination against particular regions and groups such as ethnic minorities and disabled people.[3] Poor people need to be more involved in decisions about services – whether through local councils, NGOs, trade unions or faith organisations.

6.10 Fourth, international partners, UN organisations and NGOs will need to play a more active role in providing public services in fragile states where governments are weak and direct support to governments is not yet possible. Where states are committed to providing services but lack capacity, this might mean contracting out basic services to

NGOs. Just such a move has been made in Cambodia and Afghanistan. Often, communities and local authorities can provide services even where national institutions are ineffective – and so reach poor people more quickly than would otherwise have been possible. But these arrangements need to be designed to support the long term responsibility of the state. In Afghanistan, the Government is giving small grants to community councils through the National Solidarity Programme.

6.11 By working together, international partners can help provide public services more quickly than stand-alone projects. In joint programmes such as the national AIDS programmes in Burma and Zimbabwe, pooled funding and a single plan have helped pay for the activities of a range of NGOs, while reducing burdensome procedures usually associated with multiple projects.

The UK will

- Increase spending on public services - education, health (including HIV and AIDS), water and sanitation and social protection - to at least half of the UK's direct support to developing countries.

- Make long-term commitments to partner countries through ten year plans for expanding public services.

- Provide predictable and flexible assistance to these plans using, as appropriate, either direct budget support, basic service grants (which earmark resources to one or more sector), or working through civil society, faith based or other organisations.

Getting children into school...

6.12 Our priority is to get the 100 million children of primary school age who are not currently attending school into a classroom with a teacher. Education is both a right and a route out of poverty. People who have been to school are more likely to find work, look after their health and demand that governments act in their interests. But on current trends, 67 countries will not achieve the MDG for universal primary education.[4] Urgent action is needed to increase funding, and to deal with the problems that prevent children from going to school – including the devastating effects of AIDS.[5]

6.13 School fees deter parents from enrolling their children, particularly girls. Seventy-eight out of 94 low income countries charge some type of fee for primary education.[6] When faced with a choice of paying for a son or daughter to go to school, parents will often choose the son. Countries that have abolished school fees, however, have seen a huge increase in enrolment. The UK strongly supports free primary education, and is helping governments to pay for the additional teachers and classrooms needed to cope with the growing numbers of children in school.

Learning for free

Mrisho is an eight-year-old pupil at Kerezange School on the outskirts of Dar es Salaam, Tanzania. He and his brother Benadi know how lucky they are: "My parents say that it is a blessing that they do not have to pay for us to go to school," says Mrisho. "I think so too, because if they did, my brother and I may not have been able to come to school."

6.14 Helping girls enrol and stay in school means tackling the discrimination they face. Community awareness programmes about the importance of educating girls help. More women teachers and better sanitation in schools also helps overcome some of the social barriers. This is why the UK supports the UN Girls Education Initiative, together with special projects to support girls education.

6.15 While universal primary education remains our priority, there is also a growing need to invest in secondary and higher education and vocational skills training. Young people graduating from secondary schools and colleges today will become the teachers, health workers and business people of tomorrow. Secondary education is one of the most important ways of improving the status and health of young women.

Abolishing fees helps children go to school

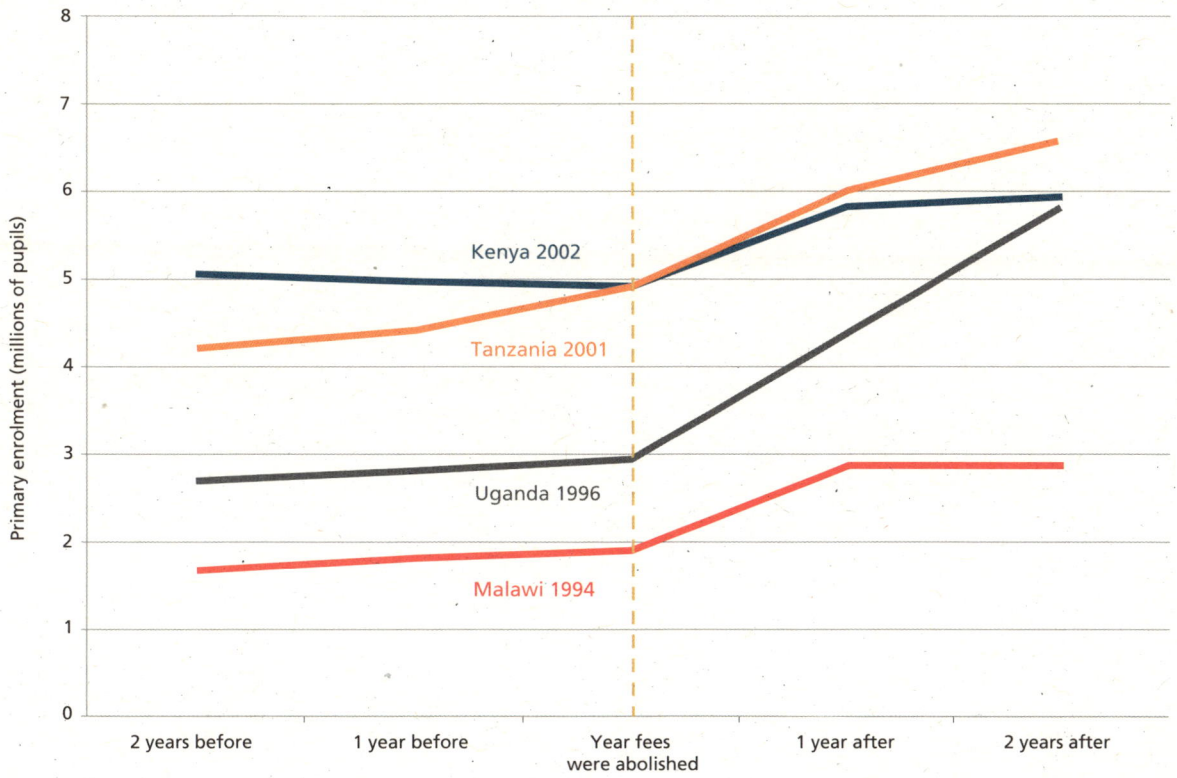

Source: UNESCO Institute for Statistics, www.uis.unesco.org

6.16 Many developing countries will need to increase their spending on education. This will require a substantial increase in aid, until the poorest countries have grown enough to support themselves. Providing a good quality education to all children of primary school age by 2015 will require an extra US$10 billion in aid each year. This will include the costs of removing school fees, dealing with the effects of AIDS, and providing school meals and grants to help poor families send their children to school.

6.17 The Education for All Fast Track Initiative (FTI), which the UK supports, estimates that by 2008 up to 60 countries will have credible plans to get all children into primary education by 2015.

Fast track to success

The Fast Track Initiative brings international partners together to support national education plans. The results so far are good. In the first seventeen countries to join the FTI, more children are completing primary school than in other similar countries. For example, in Niger only 20% of children completed primary education – one of the lowest rates in the world. Since joining the FTI in 2002, school enrolment has doubled, and completion has risen to 36%. From hiring 250 teachers a year, it is now hiring more than 2,500 a year.[7]

The UK will

- Spend at least £8.5 billion on education between 2006 and 2015, and provide long term commitments to help governments plan ahead. This will double our spending to over £1 billion a year by 2010.

- Increase our total contribution to the Education for All Fast Track Initiative from £50 million to £150 million over the next three years to help countries speed up the implementation of their education plans.

- Support the removal of user fees for primary education in all our partner countries, and help governments cope with the resulting increase in enrolment.

- Support special initiatives to get more girls into school.

- Provide new support for higher education and vocational skills training to train the professional staff needed by health and education services.

Improving health…

6.18 Too many people die of easily preventable diseases and too many suffer ill-health which stops them from earning a living. If everyone could receive basic health care, the number of children dying could be reduced by two-thirds, and the number of mothers dying by three-quarters.[8]

6.19 However, the funding gap is huge. Developing countries are short of finance, trained staff, and basic medicines. The Commission on Macro-economics and Health estimated that basic health care in poor countries can be put in place for around US$35 per person per year.[9] But spending on health in most countries is far less than this.

6.20 Developing countries therefore need to increase their own spending on health. In 2000, African Governments meeting in Abuja agreed to increase funding from an average of 8% of their budgets to 15%. However, most are far from achieving this because of other demands for expenditure.

6.21 International partners have increased their support for health significantly in recent years. There are now a number of initiatives on individual diseases, and over 70 health funds and partnerships. The Global Fund to fight Aids, Tuberculosis and Malaria and the Global Alliance for Vaccines and Immunisation have raised US$8.7 billion and US$1.7 billion respectively. The IFFIm will raise a further US$4 billion. The Joint United Nations Programme on HIV/AIDS (UNAIDS) estimate that US$8-10 billion will be spent on AIDS each year from 2005 to 2007 – but this is only about 60% of what will be needed.[10] The UK will work with others to close this financing gap and ensure that the money is used effectively.

6.22 Developing countries, bilateral agencies, UN agencies and civil society have agreed to fight AIDS through 'the three ones': one co-ordinating organisation, one plan, and one monitoring system for all external support. These principles should apply to health services more widely. Fighting stigma and discrimination, making condoms available and providing better information so people can protect themselves will be important too.

6.23 Almost all deaths as a result of pregnancy and childbirth are avoidable. Sexual and reproductive health services and rights need significant support. Action is needed to tackle social and cultural discrimination that prevents women getting information and health care, denies their freedom to choose if and when to have children, and greatly increases their vulnerability to HIV.

6.24 Strong national health services are essential to do all this. The biggest problem many countries face is not having enough doctors, nurses and support staff. This has been made even worse by AIDS, and by highly trained health professionals leaving to work in richer countries, including the UK.[11] Sub-Saharan Africa needs nearly 1.5 million more health workers. Worldwide, more than four million are needed.[12] We need to do more to invest in human resources.

Tackling the African health staff crisis

The UK will help partners to solve their staffing crises by:

- Training professional workers such as doctors, nurses, managers, pharmacists and other support staff – this includes support to higher education.

- Creating incentives for staff to work in under-served areas – for example through hardship allowances or better housing.

- Increasing support for community health workers – people who can help treat many simple illnesses and are more likely to live in the communities they serve.

- Expanding links between the UK National Health Service and poor countries.

- Exploring opportunities for health workers to return from the UK to their own countries, for extended periods, to help improve health services.

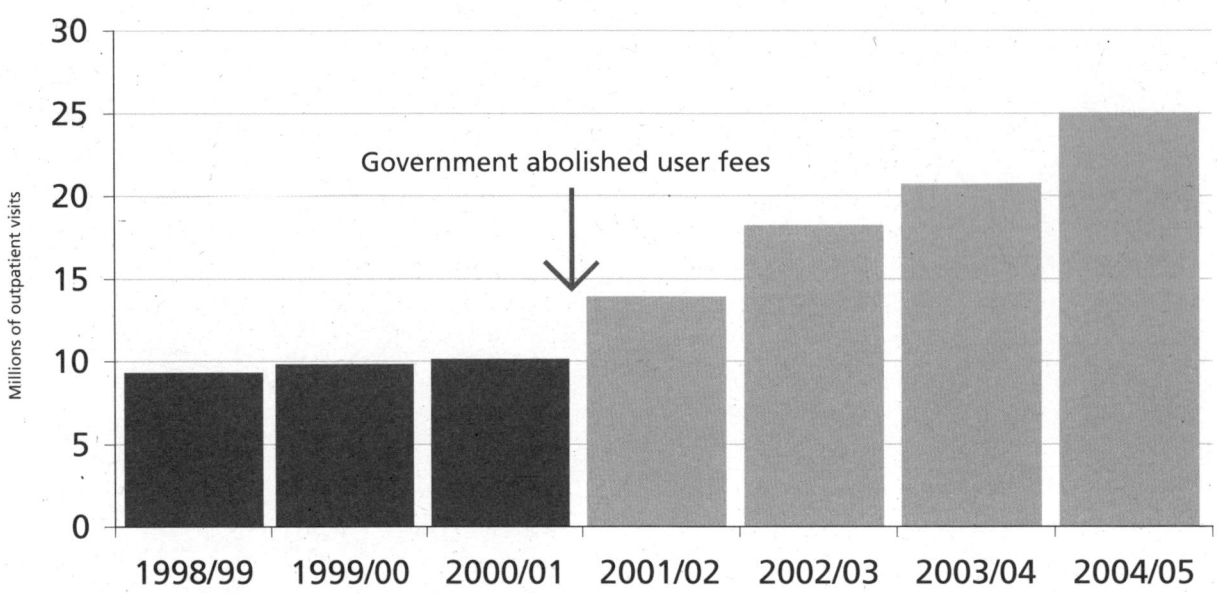

In Uganda, abolishing fees helped double attendance at health clinics

Source: Ministry of Health (2005) Annual Health Sector Performance Report for 2004/05. Kampala: Government of Uganda.

6.25 As with education, removing user fees can dramatically increase access to health services. In Uganda, abolishing fees doubled the number of people going to clinics, and more than doubled immunisation rates for children. More than 230,000 children's lives could be saved each year if fees were abolished in twenty African countries.[13]

6.26 More also needs to be done to hold service providers to account. For example, publishing local budget information can show whether more money is being spent on men's or women's health. In Nepal, South Africa and Zambia, radio dramas funded by UK aid have helped inform citizens about family health and AIDS services.

6.27 Medical research offers huge potential for improving people's lives. It has already helped eradicate smallpox, and soon polio, thanks to an easy-to-use oral vaccine. Simple treatments for diarrhoea, such as oral rehydration, have saved millions of children's lives. New artemisinin-based therapies and mosquito nets are bringing down death rates from malaria. And antiretroviral drugs are helping people with AIDS to live longer, and preventing the spread of HIV to infants at birth.

6.28 More research is needed for a new generation of drugs, vaccines and treatment methods. But the commercial incentives for undertaking research on the diseases that afflict the world's poor are weak. Globally, only 10% of the total money spent each year on health research is devoted to diseases responsible for 90% of health problems.[14] The G8 agreed to use more public-private partnerships to share the costs of developing new products. 'Advance market commitments' are a powerful way of providing guarantees that new successful vaccines will be purchased. With these incentives, there are now better prospects for malaria treatments. But more work is urgently needed on antiretroviral therapies for children with AIDS.

The UK will

- Work with developing countries to back ambitious ten year plans to improve health services, including ways of recruiting and training more doctors and nurses.

- Help partner governments abolish user fees for basic health services, and help them tackle other barriers to access, including discrimination against women.

- Implement the IFFIm which aims to save 5 million lives in the next ten years.

- Support international efforts, led by UNAIDS, to achieve the goal of universal access to comprehensive HIV prevention programmes, treatment, care and support by 2010.

- Support the long term replenishment of the Global Fund to fight AIDS, Tuberculosis and Malaria, based on improved performance on the ground.

- Support the implementation of the 2005 Global Strategic Plan to Roll Back Malaria, providing 80% of people at risk from malaria with mosquito nets and access to effective treatment by 2010; and the 2006 Global Plan to Stop TB, in order to halve the number of deaths from TB by 2015.

- Support access to sexual and reproductive health services and rights, especially for girls and women.

- As part of the doubling of our research spending, increase our funding for a new generation of drugs and vaccines against the major killer diseases, particularly through new public-private partnerships.

- Work with G8 and others to establish advance market commitments for vaccines for major diseases.

- Make a long term commitment to the new International Drug Purchase Facility.

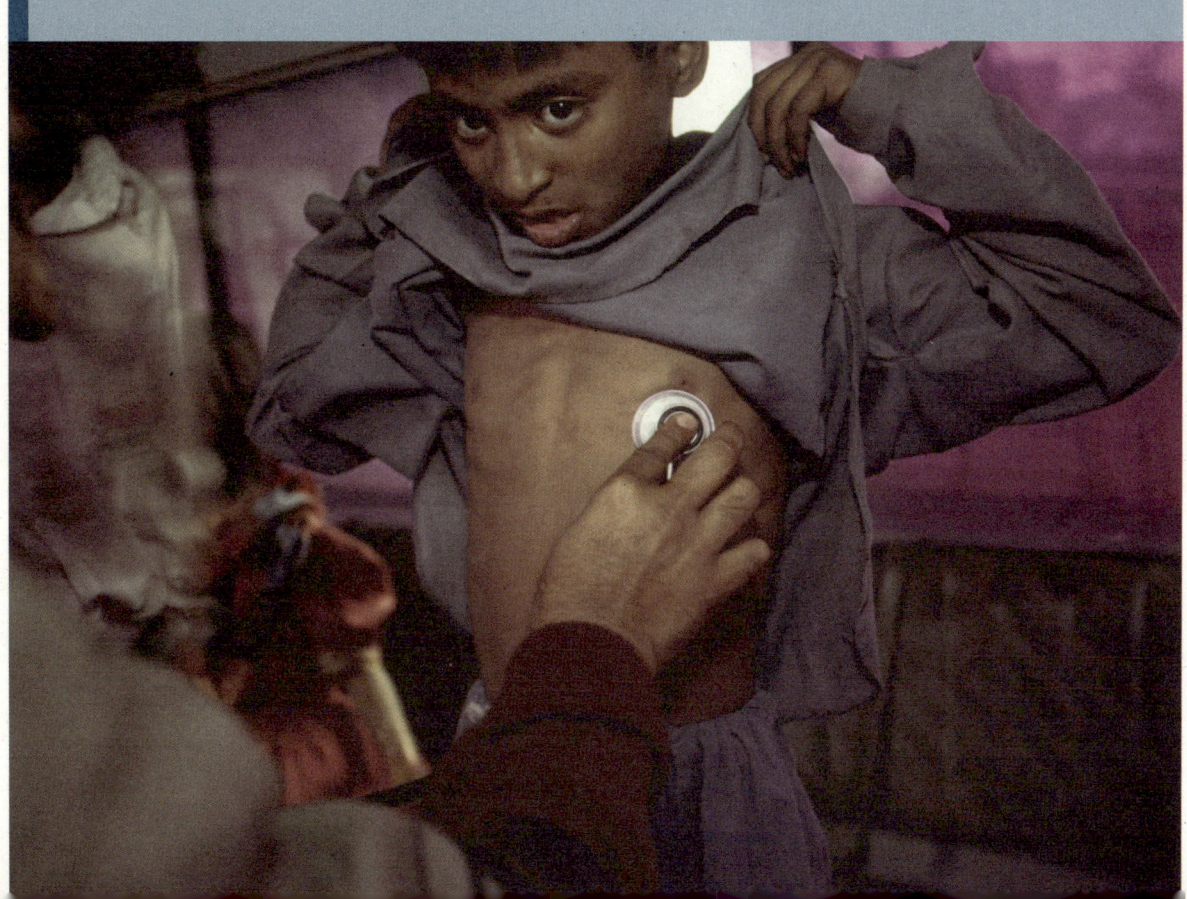

Providing clean water and sanitation…

6.29 An estimated 1.1 billion people – one in six of the world's population – have to drink unsafe water every day. As a result, about 5,000 children under the age of five die every day from diarrhoea. This will get worse as climate change reduces the amount of water available in many parts of the world. Yet despite this, many governments in developing countries do not give water and sanitation enough priority.

6.30 Far more funding is needed for water and sanitation, including maintenance.[15] This is especially the case for local government, which will have to cope with huge population growth in towns and cities. It will be particularly important to involve all sections of a community in planning and

Better water for a better life

Nana Kofi Okyere, chief of the Ghanaian village of Akim Koforidua, is delighted by how much better life has become. He points at his new village well: "This well has brought a lot of improvement. We do not have to form long queues, and children and adults do not suffer from water-borne diseases." The availability of fresh water also means the children now spend less time collecting water for their families, giving them more time to attend school. The new well is the result of a joint initiative between three organisations: Cadbury Schweppes, WaterAid (supported by DFID) and the Ghanaian farmers' co-operative, Kuapa Kokoo.

implementation in order to improve services, and to make sure that systems are well managed and maintained. Where possible, the technology used should be simple and affordable. More research is needed, for example on new technologies for water treatment and purification. Better management of water and natural disasters will also be essential – both to deal with the effect of climate change on livelihoods, and to ensure sufficient food is available at a price that people can afford.

6.31 Programmes to provide sanitation need, first of all, to create demand for it and to emphasise the responsibility of households and communities for maintenance. NGOs have a particularly important role to play here. For example, the UK has funded WaterAid in Bangladesh to develop 'Community Led Total Sanitation' to villages.

This makes sure that water, sanitation and hygiene education are provided together and with the involvement of the whole community so that everyone benefits. This new approach is now being used in other countries.

6.32 International partners are investing more in water and sanitation, but a great deal more effort and better co-ordination is needed. There are far too many partnerships and agencies with some responsibility for water – the UN alone has 23 agencies – which creates confusion.

Getting water running

In Bangladesh, the UK supports an expanding Government and United Nations Children's Fund (UNICEF) programme for rural hygiene, sanitation and water supplies which has already served 7.5 million people.

In India, we support the Government's Urban Services for the Poor Programme in 32 towns across Andhra Pradesh. It provides infrastructure in slum areas, including water supply and sanitation, for 2 million poor people.

In South Africa, the UK has supported the Government's programme to use the private sector to build and operate new water systems, before handing them over to local government. In four years this has given 4 million people better water supplies.

The UK will

- Double our assistance to water and sanitation in Africa to £95 million a year by 2007/08, and more than double funding again to £200 million a year by 2010/11.

- In Africa, focus our efforts on countries most off-track to meet the water and sanitation MDGs.

- Support the African Development Bank's Rural Water Supply and Sanitation Initiative to help achieve 80% water and sanitation coverage by 2015.

- In Asia, work directly and with others to expand water and sanitation services across the region.

- Work with civil society organisations in all regions, to help them demand better access to water and sanitation.

- Support UN Water to co-ordinate international assistance more effectively.

- As part of our doubling of research funding, significantly increase support for the development of innovative technologies for cleaner water and sanitation.

Protecting the very poorest…

6.33 There is now strong evidence that social protection – such as small but regular transfers of cash – has huge benefits for poor people.[16] Social protection reduces hunger and boosts incomes. It helps families send their children to school, helps women to use health services, and helps people with AIDS to get treatment. It injects cash into local economies, creating demand for goods and services that help small businesses grow. And it helps tackle the inequalities that trap successive generations in long-term poverty.

6.34 Social transfers in poor countries are a realistic option. The International Labour Organisation has shown that providing small cash transfers to the poorest 10% of people in most African countries would cost less than 3% of government budgets. And for sub-Saharan Africa as a whole, reaching 10% of the population would cost US$760 million each year.[17] This is just 3% of the US$25 billion of additional aid to Africa agreed by the G8 at Gleneagles.

Cash in on education

Maria and Carlos Oliveira da Silva live with their two children near the town of Formosa, in central Brazil. The family gets support from the Government's Bolsa Familia programme. This provides a monthly grant to poor families with children – on the condition that their children attend school and use local health services. "For us the best thing is the certainty," says Maria. "We know that each month we can afford to buy enough food and school supplies for our children. This means that we can plan for the future. Even when all of our chickens died, we had enough spare money to pay off our loans without selling our land."

6.35 Transfers can be made to everyone (such as a pension for all older people) or can be targeted at the very poor (such as households with orphans and vulnerable children). Communities can help identify those in need, or the providers of transfers can identify families directly. Local government and social welfare departments have a big role to play, but they often need more staff and money. And private organisations, like banks, can be highly effective at distributing transfers.

6.36 In recent years, a number of developing countries have shown that there are effective ways of providing social protection. The Ethiopian Government has established the Productive Safety Nets Programme to help over 8 million people with regular cash payments and food. This is reducing hunger, and helping families buy livestock. Countries such as Bangladesh, Brazil and Mexico have linked cash transfers for poor families to children using health and education services. In Nepal and Bangladesh, voucher schemes are helping women to access family planning. The UK supports many of these schemes, and we are working with partners in Kenya, Zambia and Pakistan to develop new ones.

The UK will

- Significantly increase spending on social protection in at least ten countries in Africa and Asia by 2009, supporting national programmes and working with the UN and NGOs in fragile states.

- Working with European partners and national governments in Africa, double to 16 million the number of people moved from emergency relief to long term social protection programmes by 2009.

- Support partnerships between developing countries to share experience of expanding social protection.

How change happens:
Getting children into school in Uganda

After the despotic rule of Idi Amin and the damaging effects of the 1979 war with Tanzania, Uganda's education system had virtually collapsed. Things began to improve after President Yoweri Museveni came to power in 1986. Primary school enrolment rose modestly from 2.2 million in 1986 to 3.1 million in 1996. But by the mid-1990s Uganda was a country heavily in debt, with little money to spend on education. Parents across the country were struggling to pay education costs equivalent to about one-fifth of an average family's income. Almost one-third of school-age children were not enrolled in school at all. And the few who were enrolled were unlikely to reach the final grade.

The Ugandan Government committed itself to tackling the problem, and in 1997 implemented a policy of Universal Primary Education which allowed children to go to school for free. This put unprecedented pressure on teachers, textbooks, classrooms and the education budget. But the Government did not give in and, supported by its international partners, increased education spending from 17.8% of recurrent expenditure in 1990 to 31% today. It recruited an additional 70,000 teachers, built 50,000 new classrooms, bought 20 million new textbooks and introduced new policies to improve efficiency, promote gender equity, tackle AIDS, and fight corruption.

The effect of introducing universal primary education was astonishing. Pupil enrolment jumped by 70% in a single year, from about 3 million in 1996 to over 5 million by 1998, and had reached 7.4 million by 2004.

working internationally to tackle climate change

chapter 7
managing climate change

> Climate change poses the most serious long term threat to development and the Millennium Development Goals.
>
> Developing countries must be part of a future solution to climate change.
>
> Developing countries will need support to adapt. The costs will be huge.

The climate is changing…

7.1 Climate change is re-shaping our world. It is a global problem, requiring a global solution. It will affect developing countries most of all because they have the least capacity to respond. All countries will need to work together to tackle global emissions of greenhouse gases, and to adapt to the impact of climate change.

7.2 The Intergovernmental Panel on Climate Change (IPCC), and a growing body of independent research, have provided overwhelming evidence that the world is getting warmer, and that human activity is primarily responsible.[1] Burning fossil fuels, like oil and coal, and the changing use of land, including the destruction of forests, have increased the atmospheric concentration of 'greenhouse gases' (mainly carbon dioxide) – so called because they keep the world warm by trapping heat from the sun.[2] In the last 150 years, greenhouse gas emissions have increased so rapidly that during the 20th century the world became warmer at a faster rate than at any point during the past 1,000 years.[3] Due to time lags in the climate system, temperatures are already set to rise by one degree celsius over the next few decades. If the world does not act now to curb emissions, average global temperatures in 2100 could be between 1.4 and 5.8 degrees higher than they were in 1990.

7.3 The greatest impact of the rising temperatures will be on the water cycle, which is a vital part of our whole climate system. The IPCC forecasts that rainfall will become less predictable over time – particularly in parts of Asia, sub-Saharan Africa and Latin America. Greater variations in rainfall, combined with rising sea levels and higher sea temperatures, are likely to lead to more frequent and more extreme weather events – such as storms, floods and droughts.[4]

7.4 In 2005, under the UK's Presidency, the G8 focused on climate change along with Africa. The G8 agreed a Plan of Action that will help developing countries to access low carbon energy and adapt to climate change; and began an 'informal dialogue' with large

Living on the edge

Abukar is a village elder who is experiencing climate change first hand. The number of droughts in the Somali region of Ethiopia has increased in the last decade, but people's ability to endure them has decreased. Abukar explains that "the droughts are killing our livestock. People are struggling to feed themselves. Because of this there have been more conflicts between tribes and even within villages. Without support from the Red Cross, human lives and livestock would have been lost."

developing countries – Brazil, China, India, Mexico and South Africa - to promote international action.

Climate change matters for development...

7.5 Many poor countries already struggle to cope with extreme weather and variations in the climate. People in the poorest countries are most reliant on environmental resources for their livelihoods.[5] These resources are already under pressure and likely to be degraded further by climate change.[6] For example, in Africa, desertification (where fertile land becomes desert) in the Sahel is already shrinking the amount of agricultural land.[7] Declining rainfall and higher temperatures in sub-Saharan Africa will significantly shorten the growing season in many countries, resulting in lower crop yields and less pasture for livestock. The poorest regions are likely to be worst affected.[8] The OECD estimates that in six developing countries alone, climate change could undermine US$1.5 billion of development assistance – for example by damaging infrastructure as sea levels rise.[9]

7.6 Climate change will undermine public health. Higher temperatures make it easier for diseases to spread. Longer rainy seasons

Climate change vulnerability in Africa

Source: Vital Climate Graphics, Africa 2002, UNEP/GRID Arendal. Cartography by UNEP/GRID-Arendal, Norway http://www.grida.no/climate.vitalafrica

Extreme weather is happening more often

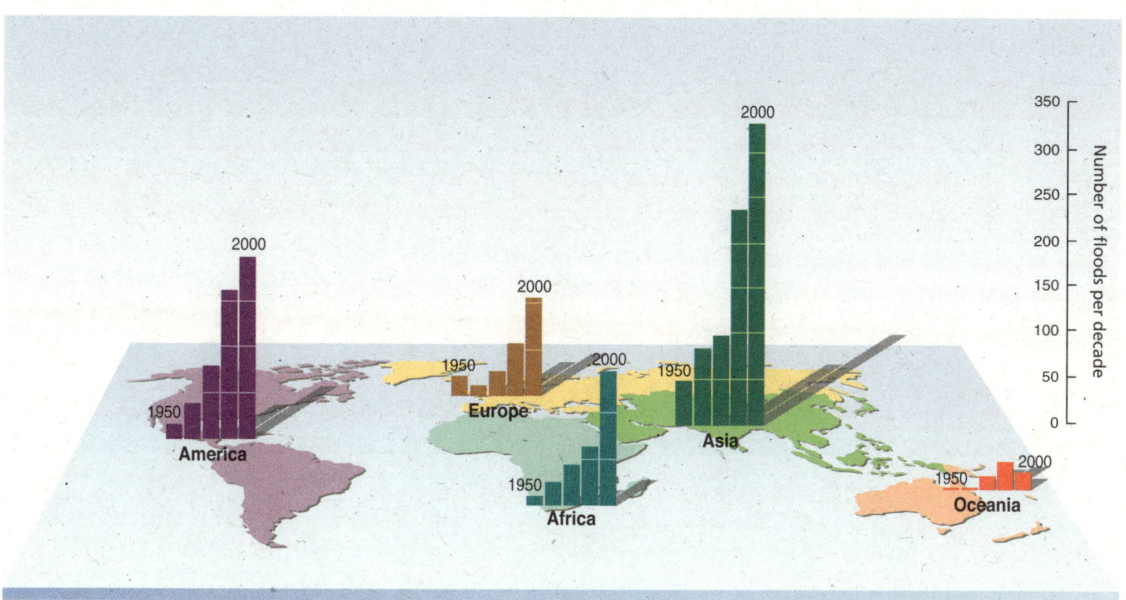

Source: UNEP (2005) Millennium Ecosystem Assessment. Cartography by Philippe Rekacewicz UNEP/GRID - Arendal and Millennium Ecosystem Assessment www.millenniumassessment.org

have already started to increase malaria in parts of Rwanda and Tanzania. The worldwide risk of catching malaria could double by 2080.[10] More frequent floods, particularly in areas of poor sanitation, increase the risk of water borne diseases such as cholera.[11] Meanwhile, retreating glaciers and less freshwater from rivers will make it more difficult to provide drinking water and sanitation.

7.7 The effect of extreme weather on poor communities is devastating. Approximately three in four natural disasters – such as droughts, floods and cyclones – are weather related.[12] Ninety-seven per cent of deaths from natural disasters occur in developing countries. Poor communities struggle to recover as disasters become more severe and more frequent. And disaster prone regions struggle to attract investment, which further undermines their development prospects. In Mozambique, torrential rainfall in 2000 led to the worst flooding in 50 years. It directly affected 2 million people and forced 650,000 to leave their homes. It cost US$600 million and reduced economic growth from a target of 10% to below 4%.[13]

Working for an international solution...

7.8 The UK is working for international agreement on urgent action to prevent dangerous climate change. Getting the whole world to agree is difficult, but it is essential nonetheless. Countries fear they will be put at an economic disadvantage if they reduce emissions ahead of their competitors. The Kyoto Protocol set targets up to 2012 for the richest countries, which have historically contributed more to emissions. But in recent years, developing countries have started to account for an increasing proportion of overall emissions. By 2025, developing countries are predicted to overtake the energy emissions of developed countries.[14] Among them, China, India, Brazil and Mexico will be the most significant although their emissions per person will still be low compared to developed countries.

7.9 In December 2005, at the Montreal UN Climate Change Conference, governments agreed to begin discussions about arrangements beyond 2012. The UK believes there is an urgent need to build a shared international understanding on the safe level of concentrations of greenhouse gases in the atmosphere – a level that will avoid dangerous climate change – and the action required to meet this. Any future agreement must ensure that developing countries, particularly the poorest, can continue to grow their economies. This will mean that as their share of global energy consumption grows, so too, initially, will their share of global emissions. And any future agreement must enable developing countries to access resources to reduce carbon emissions and help them adapt to the effects of climate change. At Gleneagles, the G8 launched an 'informal dialogue' with large developing countries in support of formal negotiations. Since 1997, the UK and other donors have helped developing countries build their capacity to negotiate on international trade. Negotiations on climate change will require a similar effort.

Who is emitting the most carbon dioxide?

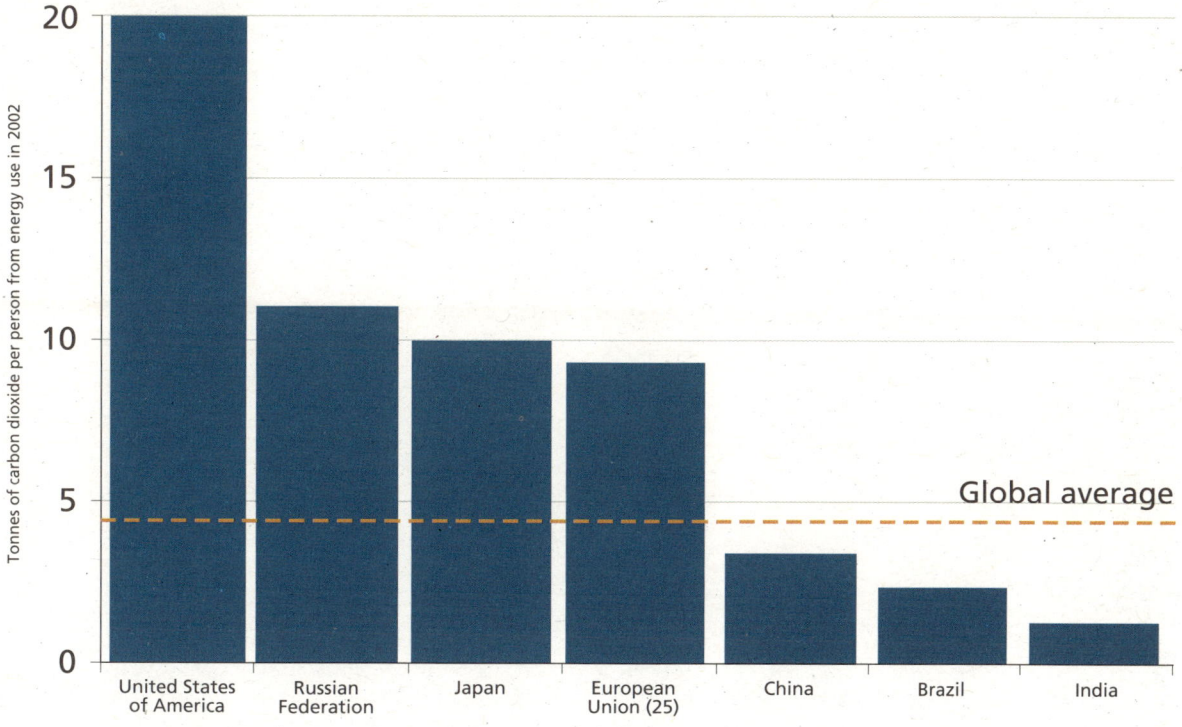

Source: World Resources Institute Climate Analysis Indicators Tool Version 3.0 (2006) www.cait.wri.org

7.10 The cheapest way of stabilising the concentration of greenhouse gases, or meeting individual targets for reducing emissions, is by trading 'carbon credits' (or emissions permits). The EU Emissions Trading Scheme is the largest regional carbon-trading scheme in the world and has the potential to become the hub of a global carbon market. Further development of international, regional or domestic schemes could help developing countries – particularly large developing countries – to reduce emissions and generate resources for cleaner energy of up to US$120 billion a year.[15]

The UK will

- Work for international agreement on:
  - A long term stabilisation goal to avoid dangerous climate change.
  - A way of reaching the stabilisation goal, which enables developing countries to grow, helps to fund the investment needed for clean energy and helps developing countries to adapt.
- Help developing countries to prepare for international discussions on a future climate change framework.
- Help developing countries take part in and benefit from mechanisms to reduce emissions, including trading schemes, as these evolve.

Changing our behaviour

Climate change is a global problem that cannot be solved by governments alone. But governments can set the framework, and can set an example. The UK has set targets to make central government offices carbon-neutral by 2012. DFID is using 100% green electricity in our UK offices, making our overseas offices greener too, and committed to offsetting carbon emissions from official air travel through a Government Carbon Offsetting Fund. In addition, DFID will set a target to reduce emissions from air travel and will publish progress against this.

Making the shift to cleaner energy…

7.11 Reliable and affordable energy, including electricity, is essential for economic growth. Access to cleaner, non-fossil fuel energy can also help oil-importing countries that are affected by high oil prices. Initial estimates put the additional cost of meeting the energy needs of developing countries with cleaner, more efficient sources at over US$40 billion a year.[16] This is well beyond the scope of current and planned aid. The UK has set up a review of the Economics of Climate Change (the Stern Review) to look at the costs and benefits of making the transition to cleaner energy in the medium to long term.[17] A long term international agreement, with a stable price for carbon, will be essential to create incentives for private sector investment. But specific action will still be needed to overcome barriers to investment in developing countries. At Gleneagles, the G8 agreed to promote greater use of clean energy. The World Bank has launched the Energy Investment Framework which could increase investment in cleaner energy by several billion dollars each year.[18]

7.12 Some technology transfer for cleaner energy is already taking place through the Kyoto Protocol, for example through the Clean Development Mechanism. This enables countries that have emissions targets to meet them by paying for equivalent reductions in developing countries. But resources are limited.[19] Proposals exist to expand the scheme and the UK is examining how we can guarantee a continued market for carbon credits up to and beyond 2012. Discussions on arrangements for the period beyond 2012 will also need to consider how more countries can get involved, and how to maximise access to resources and technology.[20]

The UK will

- Support the World Bank's Energy Investment Framework to increase private sector investment in low carbon energy and energy efficiency in developing countries.

- Work through the UN to develop mechanisms linked to international agreements on cutting emissions that maximise investment in clean energy in developing countries.

- Work with the G8 and EU to develop and use clean energy technology in developing countries.

Helping developing countries to adapt…

7.13 Adapting to the impact of climate change is already an urgent priority for some developing countries – particularly the poorest and most vulnerable. It will soon become a priority for many more. Adaptation is about reducing the risks posed

by climate change to people's lives and livelihoods. Sustainable development would help poor countries become less vulnerable. Education, health, savings and access to markets are important. Economic diversification is one of the best defences against climate shocks. But specific action to manage the impact of climate change is also needed. Adaptation and financing for adaptation should be part of developing countries' development plans, such as Poverty Reduction Strategies. The G8 has agreed to develop, with the World Bank, ways of making sure that the impact of climate change is taken into account in the design of development programmes.

7.14 Every developing country needs to know how climate change might affect poverty and economic growth, what it might cost, and the options for reducing the risk. It will be essential to understand the costs of adaptation now and the costs that will arise if no action is taken to reduce emissions ahead of negotiations on any future international agreement. For much of the developing world, these costs are currently unknown. The UN has set up funds – to which the UK has contributed £20 million over three years – to help poor countries develop strategies for adaptation. The World Bank is looking at the potential costs of adaptation and possible sources of funding.[21] As in the case of finance for cleaner energy, the costs are likely to be well beyond the scope of current and planned aid.

7.15 Countries will also need reliable records on the climate and accurate projections of climate change for adaptation. In most poor countries there is inadequate information on the climate and insufficient capacity to use it. This is particularly true of Africa. The G8 has agreed to support the Global Climate Observation System to address these gaps in Africa. But greater investment is needed to build and use better local climate information, not only in Africa but also in South Asia and other regions.

7.16 Reducing risk will mean diversifying the economy, investing in alternative crops and livestock or responding to changing disease patterns. Raising awareness about the impact of climate change, and improving consultation between all levels of government and civil society is essential. Through consultation with stakeholders, Bangladesh has prepared a National Adaptation Programme of Action to work out the implications of climate change. The Government of Bangladesh is now working with local communities to plant trees along the coast, educate children about climate change, and introduce fish that can live in inland water made more salty by rising sea levels. The Climate Change Adaptation in Africa programme will help governments develop different approaches to protect the livelihoods of the poorest people.[22]

7.17 Adapting to climate change also means finding ways to manage existing variations in the climate, and pressures on natural resources – such as water, soil and forests. For example, water resource management is already critical due to population growth, urbanisation and greater demand for water-intensive products like paper and textiles. Water supplies need to be monitored and managed to meet priorities for development – including agriculture, drinking water and sanitation. Close co-ordination is needed between different branches of government, and sometimes with neighbouring governments. And better infrastructure is needed to store and distribute water. This is particularly important in Africa where the majority of agriculture is rain-dependent and the capacity to store water is inadequate.

7.18 'Disaster risk reduction' is a crucial part of adaptation and particularly important to vulnerable communities. Natural disasters are already claiming a growing share of aid. Emergency assistance was estimated to exceed US$6 billion in 2003 – around 8% of total aid, compared to around 5% a year in the early 1990s.[23] The UN Hyogo Framework for Action aims to reduce the risk of natural disasters, and the effect they have on the lives and livelihoods of the poor, over the next ten years.[24] Implementing the Framework will mean building awareness about actions that governments and people can take, such as building hurricane-proof houses, preparing for disasters by improving early warning systems, and putting supplies and people in place to respond quickly.[25] Such investment is well worthwhile. A Tearfund study in India found that preparing for disasters was up to thirteen times more cost-effective than responding to them afterwards.[26]

The UK will

- Work with the G8 to implement the Gleneagles commitments on climate change.

- Work through the EU, UN and multilateral development banks to help developing countries work out how climate change will affect economic growth, the chances of reducing poverty, and their options for reducing risks.

- Support international efforts to generate resources to help developing countries adapt to climate change.

- Develop guidance with the multilateral development banks by 2008 to screen all development investments for the effects of climate change.

- As part of our doubling of research funding, significantly increase our support for research on identifying and adapting to the impact of climate change.

- Strengthen capacity to manage environmental assets that are important for the poor in developing countries.

- Help partner countries to develop sustainable, equitable ways of managing their water resources.

- Help developing countries reduce the impact of natural disasters on the poor, including by investing up to 10% of our response to each major natural disaster in preparing for future disasters.

How change happens: Adapting to floods in Bangladesh

For people who live on Bangladesh's many Chars - low-lying, infertile islands in the north of the country – physical disaster is a way of life. Bangladesh already suffers from the effects of climate change, and chars are acutely vulnerable to floods, which often wash away homes and kill livestock. This vulnerability is set to increase as the effects of climate change on Bangladesh become more severe. Adapting to them will become increasingly important, especially for the poor, who are often the most vulnerable.

The DFID-funded Chars Livelihoods Programme is helping to bring about physical, social and economic improvements for 6.5 million of the poorest and most vulnerable char dwellers in Bangladesh. To help cope with flooding, plinths are being built to raise houses above the 100 year flood line. 10,500 have been built to date and the number is increasing every day. Raising houses like this will save lives, help people sustain precarious livelihoods, and reduce the losses caused by frequent floods.

creating an international system fit for the 21st century

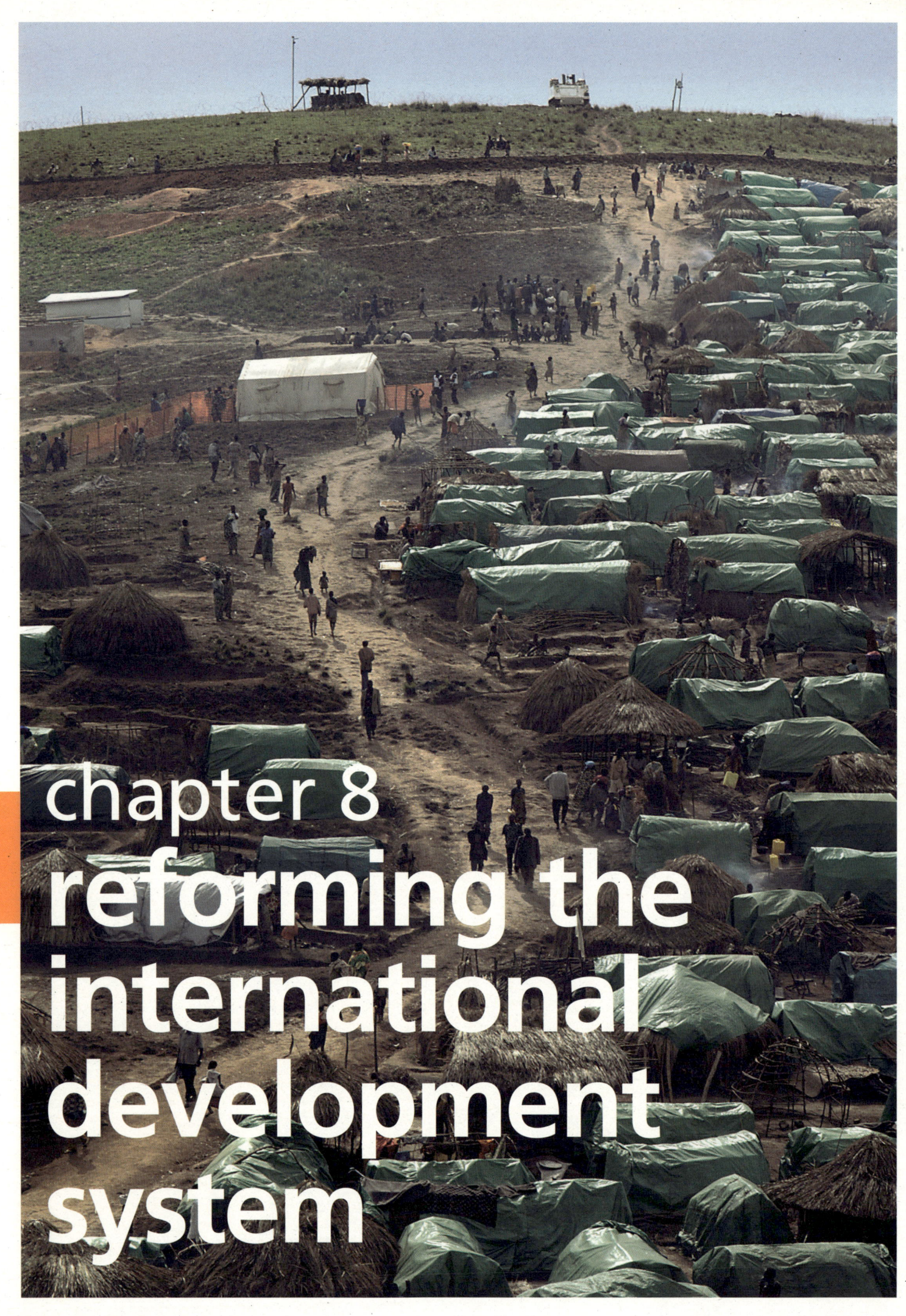

chapter 8
reforming the international development system

> **International problems need international solutions.**
>
> **Multilateral organisations have a critical role to play in delivering aid and implementing policies that work for development.**
>
> **Developing countries must have a stronger say in how the international system works.**

The international system must change…

8.1 Much of today's multilateral system – including the UN, World Bank, IMF, and the EU – was created after the terrible destruction of the Second World War. These institutions have served the world well, but the challenges we face in the 21st century are very different to those of 60 years ago.

8.2 Effective international organisations are needed now more than ever to balance competing national interests, and find solutions to problems that cannot be solved by individual countries alone. Only by working multilaterally will it be possible to: act when states fail to protect their people; enforce rules-based trade; tackle epidemics like AIDS or Avian flu that threaten us all; and manage the climate, forests, fisheries and water that we all share. There is no alternative. Without an effective international system, the world would be a more unequal, dangerous and divided place.

8.3 International organisations play a major role in delivering aid. As aid increases sharply, donors will need to rely more on multilateral channels to distribute it. Between them, just three institutions – the EC, the World Bank and the UN – already account for around 30% of global aid flows through loans, grants and technical co-operation. The UK is committed to working with others – we channel around 40% of our aid through multilateral organisations.[1]

8.4 But some parts of the international system have become either too complicated and inefficient or simply do not work at all. They must change. We will use our resources and influence to encourage reform. And in future we will use success – rather than history – as the criterion for deciding how to allocate UK funding.

8.5 This chapter sets out the changes that the UK will work for. The world needs an international development system that:

- Delivers increasing levels of development assistance effectively and shows results.

- Reflects the interests of developing countries and allows them to lead their own development.

- Holds countries (whether donors or recipients) to account for the commitments they have made to each other.

- Upholds human rights and other international standards, and takes action when these are not being met.

- Monitors progress against the targets agreed to reduce poverty.

Where do developing countries get aid from?[2]

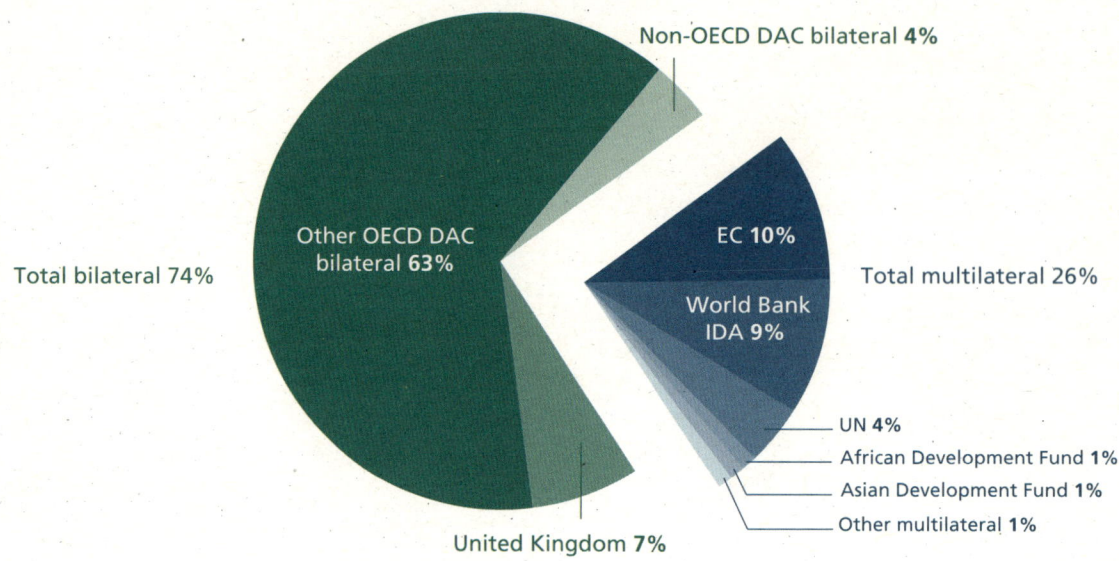

Source: OECD DAC. Total net disbursements (US$78.3 billion) of ODA to developing countries in 2004.

8.6 Significant change is needed to achieve all this. The UN's role in development needs to be radically reformed, in keeping with its unique political mandate. It should focus on providing strong political leadership in conflict and in fragile states, on setting global standards, and on helping countries agree solutions to climate change and other threats to development. The World Bank, IMF and regional development banks should help developing countries finance investments for sustainable and equitable growth and public services; and help their members manage economic shocks. To do this, they will need to reflect better the interests of all their members. And the EU should ensure that its aid is effective, and that its wider policies also support development.

8.7 The UK is strongly committed to working through the international system to reduce poverty in developing countries. We will use our resources and influence to strengthen the international system for this purpose.

Collective action in a changing world: the United Nations…

8.8 The UN's legitimacy is unparalleled. This comes from its universal membership and unique responsibilities for peace and security, sustainable development, human rights and international law. It enables the UN to agree international policies and standards that are vital for development.

8.9 The UN also provides leadership on international efforts towards the MDGs. Through its funds and programmes, the UN works to reduce child mortality, improve maternal health and achieve universal primary education. It gives advice and helps governments build their capacity to provide public services in a wide range of developing countries.

8.10 But over time, fragmentation, duplication and excessive competition for resources within the UN have reduced the impact of its development operations. The UN Secretary General has recognised the need for change, and has established a High Level Panel to identify ways to improve UN performance on

development, humanitarian assistance and the environment. The UK believes the Panel is the best chance in a generation to help the UN re-organise. Alongside this, the UK also supports enlargement of the UN Security Council, management reform and efforts to strengthen the UN's role in counter-terrorism.

8.11 We think the UN should focus more on two areas. First, it should do more to prevent conflict, broker peace, help fragile and conflict-affected states recover after crises and lead humanitarian assistance where needed. Second, it should continue to develop international agreements and standards – as it has on human rights – and push for and report progress on these.

8.12 If the UN is to do these tasks effectively, reform is needed. UN agencies and programmes must be rationalised, and merged where necessary. There should be a unified UN presence in countries – based around a single programme, with one leader, one office and one budget.

How does the UN make a difference?

- The MDGs were agreed at the UN in 2000. These eight goals have guided international development ever since. Having set the standard, the UN is helping hold countries to account for progress. In 2005 at the UN summit, world leaders re-committed themselves to achieve the MDGs by 2015.

- In 2001, 189 nations agreed a Declaration of Commitment on HIV and AIDS, an action plan to halt and reverse the AIDS epidemic. The UN is leading international efforts to help developing countries deliver their plans to tackle AIDS.

- In the DRC, the UN has helped prepare for national elections, co-ordinated the humanitarian effort, and put 16,800 peacekeepers on the ground to help create a more secure environment.

The UK will

- Urge the UN to play the leading role in fragile and conflict states.
- Seek agreement on implementing the 'four ones' in developing countries: one UN office, one leader, one programme and one budget.
- Work with other donors to reform financing by pooling funding for the UN at country level and centrally.
- Support the UN's work with the World Bank to help developing countries draw up long-term plans to achieve the MDGs.
- Support the UN in developing and implementing international standards.

Improving the international response to humanitarian crises…

8.13 Each time disaster strikes, the job of the international humanitarian system is to be there to help. Many organisations – including the UN, NGOs and the Red Cross movement – and many committed people work hard to provide assistance to people in distress.

8.14 The humanitarian system achieves a great deal, but it could be much better. As a result of climate change, it will need to respond to increasingly frequent disasters. This is one reason why the UK has argued for reform. We proposed major changes to humanitarian funding, which led to the launch of the Central Emergency Response Fund in March 2006 – the UK is the largest contributor. The Fund aims to tackle imbalances between well-funded and neglected crises, and to make money available as soon as a new crisis happens. We argued for stronger UN coordination and leadership – as is now happening in countries like Sudan and the DRC, where international partners, including the UK, have pooled funding under the UN Humanitarian Co-ordinator's leadership. And a new 'cluster system' has been established, in which different agencies have overall responsibility for nine areas of need.[3]

> ### Internally displaced people
>
> International agencies have not been able to cope with the rising numbers of Internally Displaced People (IDPs) in recent years. Responsibility for IDPs has been unclear. In Darfur, DRC, and Liberia, agencies were unable to protect IDPs, provide adequate camps or help them return home. In future, the UN High Commissioner for Refugees (UNHCR) should be responsible for IDPs as well as refugees. This means extending UNHCR's mandate and providing it with adequate funding to support IDPs as well as refugees.

8.15 The response to the Asian tsunami, the Pakistan earthquake and Niger's food crisis has shown that these reforms are making a difference. But further change is needed. This includes finding more skilled and experienced people to work in emergency situations, and better arrangements to rapidly deploy planes, helicopters and other logistics, for example in co-operation with the military. Gaps have to be filled – such as the lack of clear responsibility for internally displaced people. And the humanitarian system should be more accountable for its performance. In short, the world needs an effective international emergency service.

> ### Flights of hope
>
> Ten year old Abdullah lives in Kot, in Pakistan-administered Kashmir. In October 2005 he and his family were at home when an earthquake measuring 7.6 on the Richter scale struck. Abdullah's village is at 1,600 metres and is almost impossible to reach by road. Without the blankets and iron sheets transported by a United Nations Humanitarian Air Service helicopter flight (funded by the UK), Abdullah, his family and his neighbours would have faced a harsh winter without warmth and shelter.

The UK will

- Push for a single, integrated UN humanitarian system, with a lead role for UN Humanitarian Co-ordinators and the Office for the Co-ordination of Humanitarian Affairs.

- Invest at least £40 million a year in the Central Emergency Response Fund.

- Continue to provide substantial support to NGOs, the Red Cross movement and the UN, for humanitarian assistance.

- Promote changes to the emergency appeals process to make 'flash appeals' more realistic.

- Support the 'cluster system' whereby different agencies lead on specific issues during an emergency.

- Help 'cluster lead' agencies increase the number of experienced, skilled staff available in an emergency, and improve the availability of supplies and arrangements to move them quickly.

- Develop clear arrangements for using UK military equipment and personnel in humanitarian crises.

- Work with partners to publish an independent World Humanitarian Report to monitor how well the world responds to humanitarian crises.

- Support changes to UNHCR's mandate to include internally displaced people, and be willing to provide extra resources to support this work.

Financing development: the International Financial Institutions…

8.16 The World Bank and the IMF play a critical role in providing development assistance to poor countries, monitoring economic conditions and promoting better macro-economic management. But, if they are to remain relevant in a changing world, we believe they must reform.

8.17 Poor countries need to fund health, education and other public services and invest in infrastructure and growth. But in the poorest countries, neither government nor business can generate the finance they need. To help plug this gap, the World Bank provides around US$8 billion each year to low income countries through the International Development Association.[4] It also provides middle income countries with loans at close-to-market terms. And it plays a major role in gathering and sharing knowledge about development.

8.18 But to be more effective the World Bank must deal with three major challenges. First, as aid increases, the World Bank should play a leading role in providing more long-term, predictable funding for developing countries. The World Bank should convene 'Results and Resources Meetings' to help countries gather support for their plans to achieve the MDGs; provide flexible finance itself to help developing countries pay the wages of health staff or teachers, for example; and take the lead in managing increasing donor finance for education through the FTI. It should do more to help the private sector and support equitable economic growth, and do more in fragile states where the challenges and the needs are greatest. And – working with the IMF, regional development banks, and potential lenders – the World Bank should help ensure that debt problems do not re-emerge for the poorest countries.

Free treatment, fresh start

Mr Chen is 40 years old and lives in Hunan province, China. In 2005, he was diagnosed with tuberculosis at a local hospital. His family could not afford the cost of the treatment and Mr Chen was forced to stop working. The Chens found themselves struggling to make ends meet but a few weeks later the hospital learned about a World Bank/DFID tuberculosis project and its free treatment policy. Mr Chen received a free physical examination and treatment. The doctor insisted that Mr Chen's family was tested and discovered that his wife also had tuberculosis. The dispensary provided six months free treatment to the Chens. They are now fully recovered and can work and lead a normal life again.

8.19 Second, middle income countries are borrowing less from the World Bank and more from private markets than in the past.[5] This is because the combination of low global interest rates and the World Bank's social and environmental standards have reduced the advantages of borrowing from the World Bank. We believe these standards should not be discarded, because they protect people's rights. So the World Bank will need to find new ways to work with middle income countries as they still face major development challenges and are shaping the wider world.

8.20 Third, the World Bank should help tackle the global challenges facing developing countries – focusing urgently on a financing framework for clean energy and adaptation to climate change. And it should use its position and expertise to forge a new international framework to help developing countries tackle corruption and improve their governance.

8.21 Like the World Bank, the IMF must continue to change in order to better meet the needs of poor countries. Recent important innovations include: the new Exogenous Shocks Facility, which ensures that development is not undermined by global economic conditions; and the Policy Support Instrument that helps countries access IMF advice without borrowing from

it. In low income countries, the IMF should focus more on macro-economic policy advice, and less on structural issues like privatisation and trade liberalisation where its track record has been mixed; and provide advice to fragile states that is tailored to the challenges they face. And, in line with its recent medium term strategy, the IMF should help all developing countries plan for larger amounts of aid and help them manage their macro-economic and budgetary policies accordingly. [6]

8.22 Developing countries need more influence in the World Bank and IMF. They are weakly represented on both Boards, where voting rights are decided by financial contributions. This balance must change. Both institutions must do more to support developing country priorities and not impose economic policy conditions in areas like privatisation and trade liberalisation. And, if their members demand it, both institutions should be ready to change how members are represented, and how decisions are made – for example through greater voting rights for poor countries. There also needs to be greater transparency in the way that the World Bank and IMF operate. More World Bank analysis should be disclosed. And the practice of picking the heads of both institutions based on nationality should end – Presidents should be chosen on merit, as happened recently with the African Development Bank.

Regional approaches to regional issues…

8.23 Many regional problems are best solved at a regional level. Developing countries benefit from close economic co-operation with their neighbours, enabling them to exploit regional markets and manage shared resources.[7] The regional development banks in Asia, Africa, Latin America – and others like the Islamic Development Bank and the Kuwait Fund – are vital in their regions. They can be particularly helpful on issues like infrastructure, the spread of diseases, regional markets, cross-border investment, and access to scarce water. But the Asian and the African Development Banks, in particular, need significant organisational change to serve their members better.

8.24 Stronger regional banks would give developing countries a choice between sources of finance and advice on policy. And that choice would encourage innovation, and improve the quality of aid. But competition must not compromise economic, social and environmental standards. To guarantee this, the UK believes the World Bank and regional development banks (and other international financial institutions such as the European Investment Bank) should agree ground rules with each other to govern their lending operations.

8.25 Regional political organisations also matter. The AU is beginning to prove Africa's determination to deal with Africa's problems – particularly through its Peace and Security Council, the African Peer Review Mechanism, and action on migration. Similarly, Asian countries want more progress on regional integration and co-operation. The Association of South East Asian Nations and South Asian Association (ASEAN) for Regional Co-operation (SAARC) are setting up free trade agreements in East and South Asia, and there is growing political support for more regional co-operation on energy, environment and infrastructure issues.

Working beyond borders

The Asian Development Bank has supported the countries of the Mekong region (Cambodia, Lao PDR, Myanmar, Thailand and Vietnam) since 1992. The Greater Mekong Subregion Economic Co-operation Programme helps make sure that shared natural resources are well managed, tackles health and social issues, makes transport across borders easier, lays modern roads, telecommunication and power links, and promotes tourism and investment.

The UK will

- Press the World Bank to be more effective and responsive to developing country priorities; and adapt its aid instruments to better suit the differing needs of low and middle income countries.

- Encourage the World Bank and IMF to do more to help countries cope with economic shocks, corruption, and to respond to trends such as climate change.

- Encourage the multilateral and regional development banks to develop guidelines that ensure they do not compromise on economic, social and environmental standards, when they compete with each other for business.

- Press the World Bank, IMF and others to avoid economic policy conditionality in such areas as privatisation and trade liberalisation.

- Encourage the IMF and World Bank to help developing countries manage the macro-economic consequences of larger aid flows.

- Press the World Bank, IMF and regional development banks to ensure that any new lending to poor countries is consistent with the 'debt sustainability framework'.

- Support developing country calls for a stronger say at the World Bank and IMF.

- Seek transparent, competitive selection processes for the heads of all international development agencies – including the World Bank and IMF and UN – to ensure the best candidates are appointed, regardless of nationality.

- Work with others to strengthen the African and Asian regional development banks, especially for regional and cross-border infrastructure.

- Work with others to support AU, SAARC, ASEAN and other regional efforts to address regional issues critical for growth and poverty reduction.

A new alliance for development: the European Union…

8.26 The EU is now more important for development than ever. The EU acts politically, makes policies that matter for developing countries and spends 55% of the world's aid money.[8] The UK is committed to working more closely with EU member states and the EC on international development policy.

8.27 EU expansion has brought stability to Europe. In countries that aspire to join, political dialogue, European aid and the prospect of EU membership are leading to rapid change.[9] And the EU has significant political and economic relationships with developing countries in Africa, the Caribbean and the Pacific, Europe's 'neighbourhood', and with influential middle income countries.

8.28 Common European policies on issues like trade, agriculture, migration, climate change and security have significant implications for developing countries. Recognising this, the Council of EU Member States and the EC have agreed to report every two years on the impact of EU policy on development.[10] We will work closely with EU member states to tackle international corruption, and take forward EITI and other such initiatives.

8.29 By 2010, nearly 80% of the new aid promised in 2005 will come from European Member States.[11] Decisions made in Europe will determine how effectively that money is used. And Europe's influence in shaping aid policy is growing. The European Consensus on Development, agreed in 2005, united Europe – Member States and the EC – for the first time behind a shared view of development co-operation. The Consensus is clear that: the primary objective of European aid is eradicating poverty; the poorest countries should get priority; developing countries should 'own' the development process; EU Member States should increase and harmonise their aid; and the EU's wider policies should support development.[12] The challenge now is to make sure that these principles are applied in practice in all countries receiving EC aid.[13]

8.30 After five years of reform, EC aid is now much better than it was. EuropeAid was set up to implement all external assistance, replacing the previous fragmented system. Management of aid has been largely decentralised to the field. And the European Development Fund, which supports African, Caribbean and Pacific countries, has become more effective and flexible.[14] Europe's humanitarian work is highly respected. And new, streamlined 'instruments' for the EC's aid to different regions and themes will be in place by 2007.[15]

8.31 But to realise Europe's potential as a leader on international development, we believe more change is needed to improve co-operation between EU donors, and to make EC aid more effective. Policy and implementation of aid remains split between different parts of the Commission. And field offices have less responsibility and capacity than they need. If performance does not improve, a second wave of reform will be needed.

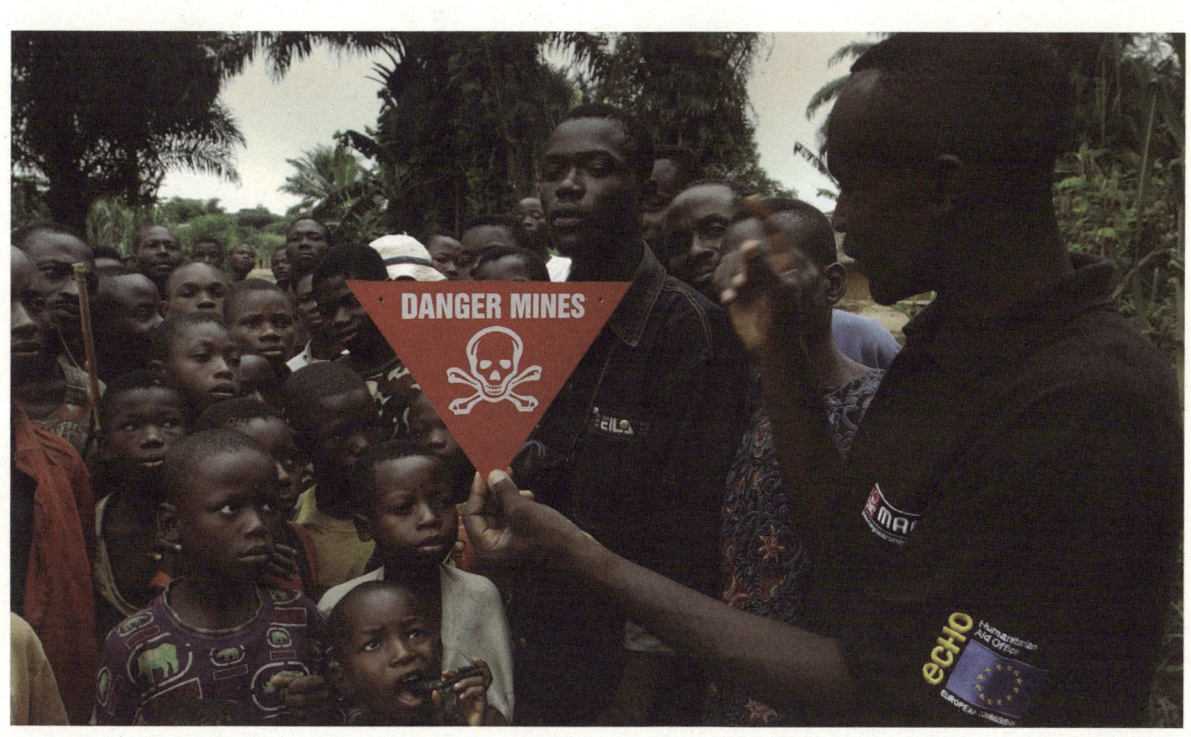

Europe makes a difference to development

- EU aid helps tackle poverty. In Burkina Faso, the EC's Euros 125 million budget support (2002-05) has helped increase primary education enrolment by over 25% since 2000, and doubled vaccination rates for measles and yellow fever since 1998. In Nicaragua, the EC's Euros 11 million water project has helped repair 145 kilometres of pipes, built over 100 wells, and helped 10,000 homes to improve hygiene standards.

- EU Member States - the UK, Spain, Italy and France and Sweden - launched the IFFIm which could save 10 million lives.

- The EU is using its bilateral partnerships to foster sustainable development in countries such as China and India, for example through the EU-China 'clean coal' initiative, launched in 2005.

- The EU has provided Euros 300 million through its Peace Facility for peace support operations in Africa in 2004-2007, particularly in Darfur, helping put thousands of African Union peacekeepers on the ground.

The UK will

- Work with others for further reform of European development assistance and institutions, so that the EU can play a leading international role on development.

- Work closely with EU Member States to implement the EU Development Policy Consensus, covering commitments on aid and wider international policies.

- Develop more joint strategies and seek opportunities for co-financing with the EC and EU Member States, wherever appropriate.

- Work with the EU as the main partner for our development aims in the 'Accession' and 'Neighbourhood' countries, and as an important partner to further development objectives in middle income countries.

- Work more closely with EU Member States to increase our influence in international development organisations.

Holding each other to account...

8.32 Aid relationships are, by nature, unequal. If developing countries are to lead their own development, they must have more authority to ensure that the international development system responds to their needs.

8.33 Within developing countries, governments need to be clear about what they want. Tanzania and Mozambique, for example, have set out clearly how they want to work with their international partners.[16] These arrangements should not be the exception but normal practice. And there should be better arrangements at the international level, for international partners and developing countries to hold each other to account for delivering their commitments.

8.34 International partners must find ways of working together to make aid better. The Paris Declaration on Aid Effectiveness – agreed in March 2005 – made clear that aid works better where:

- Developing countries determine their own policies and programmes ('ownership').
- Donors provide long term, predictable support based on local needs and priorities, and use developing countries' institutions and procedures rather than building their own parallel systems ('alignment').
- Donors reduce the burdens on developing country governments – for example by reducing the number of individual projects and administrative requirements and by 'untying' aid ('harmonisation').[17]
- Donors and developing countries focus on making the most difference to the lives of poor people ('managing for results').

Better aid for Sudan

In Juba, South Sudan, the UK is working with the Netherlands, Norway, Denmark and Sweden in a Joint Donor Team to support development in the south following the Sudan peace agreement. The new office (above) combines the bilateral programmes of the five countries into one operation. The aim is to create a fully harmonised programme to make it easier for the Government of South Sudan to manage aid, and to make aid work better. The Dutch are leading the initiative, and have provided a joint office which is staffed by a combined team from all five partners.

- Donors and developing countries hold each other to account for their promises ('mutual accountability').

8.35 There are now good examples of bilateral and multilateral partners working together in this way. The UK already pools funding with other donors in more than twenty countries, has joint strategies with other donors in six countries and joint offices in two more. But there are still too many donors with different spending and monitoring requirements. The UK believes that we, and other international partners, need to make faster progress to meet our commitments under the Paris Declaration, especially as aid increases.

8.36 The UK would like to see an independent organisation monitoring aid commitments, allocations and performance. This would significantly increase accountability. The OECD DAC – which has traditionally collected and published statistics on aid and developed guidelines for OECD members – could do this. But this will mean strengthening its capacity, and working much more closely with new non-OECD donors such as India and China.

8.37 We also need to overcome the unequal way in which aid is currently distributed. Countries often receive different amounts of aid regardless of their poverty or population size. This is partly because bilateral partners have stronger commitments to some countries than others for political or historical reasons. The result is that some countries are under-aided. The DAC should highlight where this is the case. The UK will work with others to agree a mechanism to resolve this problem, probably involving multilateral donors balancing out aid flows.

Aid is not distributed evenly [18]

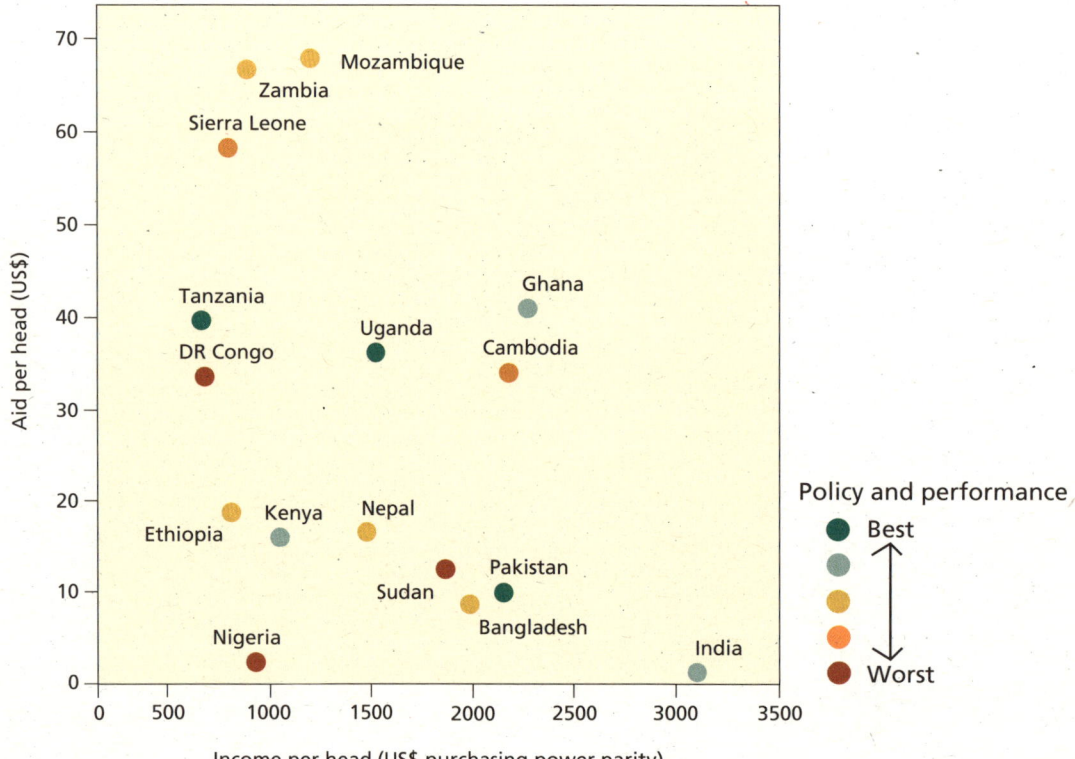

Source: ODA per capita 2000-04 average from OECD-DAC and World Development Indicators (WDI); GNI per capita 2004 from WDI; Policy and performance from World Bank CPIA 2004.

The UK will

- Work with others to implement the Paris Declaration.
- Participate in multi-donor arrangements in all developing countries by 2010 where we have a bilateral programme.
- Work with others to create arrangements for international partners and developing country governments to monitor their commitments to each other.
- Push for a stronger role for the OECD DAC in monitoring and holding international partners to account on their commitments, and in leading debate on how aid is allocated overall.
- Encourage the OECD DAC to work more closely with new non-OECD donors such as India and China.
- Support developing country efforts to manage their relationships with donors more actively so that they lead their own development effort.
- Encourage civil society and other organisations to monitor international donor performance in developing countries.

How change happens: Poverty Reduction Strategies

In 1999 the World Bank and IMF came up with a new approach to help developing countries. In order to qualify for debt relief under the HIPC, countries were asked to prepare Poverty Reduction Strategies (PRSs), to set out their priorities for development and to explain how aid and debt relief would be used to benefit the poor.

Almost all international partners now support the PRS approach, and many – including the UK – have put them at the heart of their development assistance. This is much better than multiple donors working to different objectives. PRSs have helped put the fight against poverty at the centre of the public policy debate in developing countries. This has improved the quality of their budgets and financial management, and raised the level of public spending to tackle poverty. For example, Ghana increased its expenditure on poverty reduction through its PRS from 4.8% of GDP in 2002 to 8.3% in 2005. This allowed the government to hire 10,000 additional teachers and boost primary school enrolment from 81% to 92% of children.[19] The economy also grew at rate of 5.2% in 2003 and 5.8% in 2005. Forty-nine countries have now drawn up PRSs.

9.1 Eliminating world poverty is a job for everyone, not just governments. In 2005, people all around the world raised their voices to demand change. Many people will have a direct role to play in helping deliver the commitments we have set out in this White Paper. NGOs will help deliver services, especially in fragile states. Businesses will need to invest and create jobs. Parliament and civil society groups will hold the Government to account in the UK, and encourage their counterparts in developing countries to do the same.

9.2 But eliminating world poverty is not just about people who work on development. For most people, development is not their day job. Nevertheless, in today's increasingly interconnected and interdependent world, our lives in the richest countries are affected by what happens in developing countries, and we also have an impact on the lives of people there. Making progress in the fight against poverty will mean harnessing this relationship. And the best way to make a difference – to understand how poor people live and how to turn seemingly impossible problems into manageable tasks – is to get involved.

Seeing development for yourself

Jon Snow, a Voluntary Service Overseas (VSO) volunteer as a young man and now presenter of Channel 4's evening news, had his life changed by his first visit to a developing country. "I had never been on a plane, and had only once been out of England. Yet suddenly here I was standing in the tropical sun, next to a couple of rusting customs sheds at Entebbe airport in Uganda. I was waiting for a priest in an old Volkswagen who would drive me the 200 miles to the school in the bush, on the banks of the Nile, where I was to teach for the next twelve months. VSO and Uganda have informed my life ever since. I only became a journalist to find a way back to Africa."[1]

9.3 There are many ways to do this. Schools, universities, clubs, churches, temples and mosques can debate the issues, generate new ideas, and ultimately influence opinion. And people can help organisations that need their skills. A link between Nottingham City Hospital and Jimma University Teaching Hospital in Ethiopia, for example, has helped build capacity for better nursing, midwifery and management training. Links between schools can help children learn and help each other, and change the way they see the world. Links between trade unions can help build capacity. Volunteers – whether they are campaigning in this country or sharing skills in developing countries – can affect the lives of hundreds of people. In times of crisis or disaster, people can give money, volunteer their time in the UK, or in the affected area if they have specialist skills.

The UK will

- Double our investment in development education, as we seek to give every child in the UK the chance to learn about the issues that shape their world.

- Set up a scheme to help other groups – such as faith groups, community groups, local government, business and charitable organisations – build links with developing countries.

- Expand opportunities for young people and diaspora communities to volunteer in developing countries.

- Support internship programmes for young people to work with NGOs.

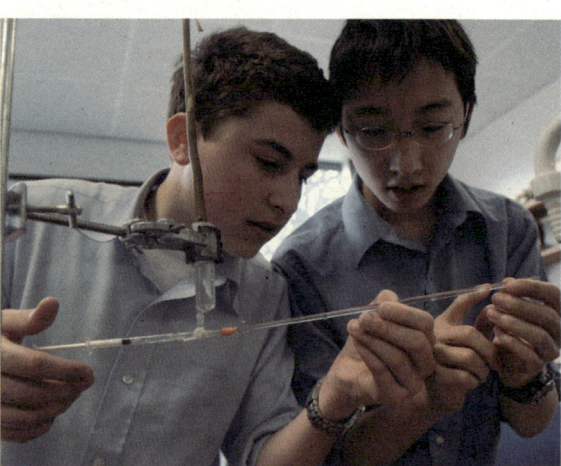

The world in your classroom

Dornton House School in Sevenoaks is partnered with the Milton Margai School for the Blind in Freetown, Sierra Leone. Both schools are working to broaden the experience of blind and partially sighted young people. Students have been exchanging Braille letters, and some have formed lasting friendships. And the schools are looking together at how to deal with conflict. Dornton House is just one of many schools in the UK that are using the 'Global Dimension' to teach our children about the world they live in.[2]

9.4 Everyday choices matter too. In 2004, DFID and the Rough Guide launched 'The Rough Guide to a Better World', setting out how you can use your money, time and influence to change the world – giving to charities, buying fairly traded products and goods made without child labour, taking part in local campaigns and events. All these actions raise money for good causes. But they also help build commitment to change, and make that change happen.

To get further information on how you can make a difference, go to www.dfid.gov.uk

glossary

AU	African Union
AIDS	Acquired Immune Deficiency Syndrome
ASEAN	Association of South East Asian Nations
DFID	Department for International Development
DRC	Democratic Republic of Congo
EC	European Commission
ECOWAS	Economic Community of West African States
EFA	Education for All
EU	European Union
EITI	Extractive Industries Transparency Initiative
FCO	Foreign and Commonwealth Office
FTI	Fast Track Initiative
G8	Group of 8 most industrialised countries
GDP	Gross domestic product
GNI	Gross national income
HIV	Human Immunodeficiency Virus
IBRD	International Bank for Reconstruction and Development
ICF	Investment Climate Facility
IDA	International Development Association
IDPs	Internally displaced people
IFF	International Finance Facility
IFFIm	International Finance Facility for Immunisation
IMF	International Monetary Fund
IPCC	Inter governmental Panel on Climate Change
MDGs	Millennium Development Goals
NEPAD	New Partnership for Africa's Development
NGO	Non-governmental organisations
ODA	Official development assistance
OECD DAC	Development Assistance Committee of the Organisation of Economic Co-operation and Development
PRS	Poverty Reduction Strategies
SAARC	South Asian Association for Regional Co-operation
SARS	Severe Acute Respiratory Syndrome
TB	Tuberculosis
UN	United Nations
UNAIDS	Joint United Nations Programme on HIV/AIDS
UNCAC	United Nations Convention Against Corruption
UNEP	United Nations Environment Programme
UNESCO	United Nations Educational, Scientific and Cultural Organisation
UNHCR	United Nations High Commission for Refugees
UNICEF	United Nations Children's Fund

endnotes

Chapter 1
Delivering the promises of 2005

1. World Bank (2006) World Development Indicators 2006. Washington DC: World Bank.

2. The Commission for Africa was formed in 2004 at the invitation of the Prime Minister. It consisted of seventeen eminent people (nine of them Africans) from all over the world, and their report 'Our Common Interest: Report of the Commission for Africa' was launched in 2005, containing ideas and recommendations for action by G8, EU, and African leaders and international institutions.

3. Gleneagles, Perthshire, was the location for the G8 Summit in 2005, under the UK Presidency. At the Summit, discussions were held on Africa between the G8 leaders and seven African leaders (from South Africa, Algeria, Nigeria, Ethiopia, Tanzania, Ghana and Senegal), and on climate change between the G8 leaders and the leaders of five developing country economies (China, India, Mexico, Brazil and South Africa). The outcome of the Summit, including the Chair's Summary of the discussion can be found at www.g8.gov.uk.

4. Foreign and Commonwealth Office (2006) Active Diplomacy for a Changing World: The UK's International Priorities. London: Her Majesty's Stationery Office. Sustainable development aims to enable all people throughout the world to satisfy their basic needs and enjoy a better quality of life, without compromising the quality of life of future generations. See Department for Environment, Food and Rural Affairs (2005) Securing the Future – UK Government Sustainable Development Strategy. London: Her Majesty's Stationery Office.

5. World Bank (2006) Global Economic Prospects: Economic Implications of Remittances and Migration. Washington DC: World Bank.

6. UNESCO (2006) Education For All Global Monitoring Report. Paris: UNESCO.

7. World Bank (2006) Global Monitoring Report: Strengthening Mutual Accountability – Aid, Trade and Governance. Washington DC: World Bank.

8. The Millennium Development Goals are a series of targets for development that 189 countries signed up to in 2000, and re-committed themselves to at the World Summit in September 2005. They are unique in that they represent a consensus for development agreed by both developed and developing countries, and which define poverty in more than just monetary terms.

9. UNAIDS/WHO (2005) AIDS Epidemic Update. New York: UNAIDS.

10. WHO (2005) The World Health Report 2005 – make every mother and child count. Geneva: WHO. Maternal mortality estimates from the year 2000 from UNICEF (2005) Childhood under Threat. The State of the World's Children. New York: UNICEF.

11. Although the water MDG target is on track in Asia this masks problems with water quality and proper maintenance of infrastructure for safe water. See UN World Water Assessment Programme (2006) Water, A shared responsibility. The United Nations World Water Development Report 2. New York and Paris: UNESCO/Berghann Books.

12. World Bank (2006) Global Economic Prospects: Economic Implications of Remittances and Migration. Washington DC: World Bank.

13. Klasen, S. (2005) Pro-Poor Growth and Gender. What can we learn from the Literature and the OPPG Case Studies? Unpublished discussion paper for the Operationalising Pro-Poor Growth Working Group including the World Bank and the Department for International Development.

14. Chronic Poverty Research Centre (2005) The Chronic Poverty Report 2004-05. Manchester: The Chronic Poverty Research Centre.

15. World Development Indicators used in DFID (2005) Why we need to work more effectively in fragile states. DFID: London.

16. DFID calculations based on World Bank estimates in World Bank (2006) Global Economic Prospects: Economic Implications of Remittances and Migration. Washington DC: World Bank.

17. A Middle Income Country is defined by the OECD Development Assistance Committee as a country with Gross National Income per capita of between US$826 – US$10,065 in 2004, compared to less than US$825 for low income countries. DAC List of ODA recipients.

18. Our policy towards the Overseas Territories is guided by the objectives and commitments of the 1999 Overseas Territories White Paper, and the earlier International Development White Papers. The International Development Act includes an enabling provision for DFID to fulfil this role, as a specific exception to its poverty reduction remit.

19. UNICEF/WHO (2005) World Malaria Report. New York: UNICEF.

20. Commission for Africa, taken from IMF (2004) The Fund's Support of Low-Income Member Countries: Considerations on Instruments and Financing, paper prepared by the Finance and Policy Development and Review Departments of the IMF, Washington DC.

21. Commission for Africa taken from Clemens, M. Radelet, S. and Bhavani, R. (2004) 'Counting Chickens when they hatch: the short-term effect of aid on growth.' Washington DC: Centre for Global Development.

22. Commission for Africa. For every US$1 in aid, an equivalent of US$0.4 worth of domestic investment is induced that might otherwise have left as capital flight. Collier, P. and Dollar, D. (2004) Development Effectiveness: What have we learnt? Economic Journal 114:244-271. In a typical developing country, receiving aid at 2% of GDP, an additional 1% of GDP is associated with an extra 0.9% of gross investment.

23. Studies cited in Clemens, M. Radelet, S. and Bhavani, R. (2004) 'Counting Chickens when they hatch: the short-term effect of aid on growth.' Washington DC: Centre for Global Development.

24. World Bank (2006) Global Monitoring Report: Strengthening Mutual Accountability – Aid, Trade and Governance. Washington DC: World Bank.

Chapter 2
Building effective states and better governance

1. Kaufmann, D. (2004) Human Rights and Governance: The Empirical Challenge. Unpublished paper. Washington DC: World Bank Institute.

2. Sen, A. (1981) Poverty & Famines: An Essay on Entitlement and Deprivation. Oxford: Clarendon Press.

3. Mcleod, D. (2005) Review of Drivers of Change Country Study Reports. Unpublished report. UK: DFID

4. Adapted from World Bank (2004) World Development Report: Making Services Work for the Poor. New York: Oxford University Press.

5. Palley, T.I. (2003) 'Lifting the Natural Resource Curse'. Foreign Service Journal. December.

6. Direct Budget Support is when funds are provided directly to partner governments to spend using their own financial management and accountability systems, in support of poverty reduction programmes.

7. International Development Department and Associates (2006) Joint Evaluation of General Budget Support (1994 - 2004): Synthesis Report on behalf of 24 members of the Development Assistance Committee of the OECD. Glasgow: DFID. And Organisation for Economic Co-operation and Development (2005) Paris Declaration on Harmonisation and Aid Effectiveness. Paris: OECD.

8. Jenkins, R. and Goetz, A.M. (1999) 'Accounts and Accountability: Theoretical Implications of the Right-to-Information Movement in India.' Third World Quarterly 20(3): 603-22.

9. Utstein Anti-Corruption Resource Centre: www.u4.no

10. International Development Association and International Monetary Fund (2005) 'Update on the Assessments and Implementation of Action Plans to Strengthen Capacity of HIPCs to Track Poverty-Reducing Public Spending'. Unpublished paper. April.

Chapter 3
Supporting good governance internationally

1. Global Witness (2004) Same Old Story: A Background Study on Natural Resources in the DRC. Washington DC: Global Witness Publishing Inc.

2. OECD (2005) Annual Report on the OECD Guidelines for Multinational Enterprises. Paris: OECD Publishing.

3. SwissInfo 13 April 2006 and BBC News 19 December 2003.

4. Africa All Party Parliamentary Group (2006) The Other Side of the Coin: The UK and Corruption in Africa. London. March.

5. Transparency International (2002) Bribe Payers Index. www.transparency.org/policy_research/surveys_indices/bpi

Chapter 4
Promoting peace and security

1. This counts only conflicts with at least 25 battle-related deaths where one of the parties was a state, rather than wider human insecurity. Human Security Centre, University of British Columbia (2005) Human Security Report: War and Peace in the 21st Century. Canada: Oxford University Press.

2. UN Millennium Project (2005) Investing in Development. A Practical Plan to Achieve the Millennium Development Goals. New York: Earthscan.

3. Internal conflict is the most important cause of displacement. The other main causes are government repression and cross-border conflict. Norwegian Refugee Council (2005) Internal Displacement, Global Overview of Trends and Developments in 2005. Geneva: The Internal Displacement Monitoring Centre.

4. Coglan, B. and others (2006) Mortality in the Democratic Republic of Congo: a nationwide survey. The Lancet, Volume 367, Issue 9504.

5. Department for International Development (2005) Fighting Poverty to Build a Safer World. A Strategy for Security and Development. UK: DFID

6. Shows conflicts that involve a government and result in 25 or more battle deaths.

7. Centre for International Co-operation and Security, Department of Peace Studies (2005) Spending to Save: Is Conflict Prevention Cost-effective? UK: University of Bradford.

8. Islamic Republic of Afghanistan (2006) Afghanistan National Development Strategy: An Interim Strategy for Security, Governance, Economic Growth and Poverty Reduction.

9. United Nations (2004) A more secure world: our shared responsibility. Report of the Secretary General's High Level Panel on Threats Challenges and Change. The United Nations Department of Public Information.

10. The Inter Governmental Authority on Development is a sub-regional organisation which includes Djibouti, Eritrea, Ethiopia, Kenya, Somalia, Sudan and Uganda.

11. WSP International Somali Programme. WSP International is an international organisation specialising in conflict management.

12. Centre on International Co-operation (2006) Annual Review of Global Peace Operations. Lynne Rienner Publishers.

13. World Bank (2003) Breaking the Conflict Trap: Civil War and Development Policy. Washington DC: World Bank and Oxford University Press.

Chapter 5
Reducing poverty through economic growth

1. World Bank (2006) MDG website. www.ddp-ext.worldbank.org/ext/GMIS/home

2. World Bank (2006) Global Economic Prospects.

3. GDP per capita, purchasing power parity (constant 2000 international US$).

4. World Bank, International Finance Corporation (2006). Doing Business in 2006. http://www.doingbusiness.org/documents/DoingBusines2006_fullreport.pdf

5. Djankov, S. McLeish, C. and Ramlho, C. (2005). Regulation and Growth. World Bank

6. Briceño-Garmendia, C. Estache, A. and Shafik, N. (2004) Infrastructure Services In Developing Countries: Access, Quality, Costs and Policy Reform. World Bank Policy Research Working Paper 3468, December.

7. Hazell, P. and Hojjati, B. (1995) Farm / non-farm linkages in Zambia. Journal of African Economies 4(3):406-435

8. Asian Development Bank, World Bank and Department for International Development (2006) Asia 2015. Promoting Growth, Ending Poverty. 6-7 March 2006. Conference Report. UK: DFID.

9. Department for International Development Financial Deepening Challenge Fund: Strategic Project Review. Unpublished report.

10. International Finance Corporation, SME Department,(2005). Micro, Small and Medium Enterprises: A Collection of Published Data. Washington DC: IFC.

11. World Bank (2006) 'Where Is the Wealth of Nations? Measuring Capital for the XXI Century'. Conference Edition. Washington DC: World Bank.

12. Asian Development Bank, World Bank and Department for International Development (2006) Asia 2015. Promoting Growth, Ending Poverty. 6-7 March 2006. Conference Report. UK: DFID.

13. Bass, S. and Steele, P. (2006) 'Managing the Environment for Development and to Sustain Pro-poor Growth'. Institute of Development Studies and ODI.

14. IPCC (2001) Climate Change 2001: Synthesis Report. A Contribution of Working Groups I, II, and III to the Third Assessment Report of the Integovernmental Panel on Climate Change. Cambridge University Press.

15. Department of Trade and Industry (2004) Making Globalisation a Force for Good. Trade and Investment White Paper 2004. London: Her Majesty's Stationery Office.

16. The Commission for Africa (2005) Our Common Interest – An Argument. London: Penguin p.256. citing World Trade Organisation 2003.

17. The Commission for Africa (2005) Our Common Interest – An Argument. London: Penguin p.262. citing UN Comtrade.

18. HM Treasury and Department of Environment, Food and Rural Affairs (2005) A Vision for the Common Agricultural Policy.

19. Figures for aid to domestic agriculture are an OECD producer support estimate for 2004, which measures the costs of all policies and transfers that maintain domestic prices above world levels. Figures for official development assistance (ODA) are net ODA for DAC countries in 2004, including contributions to multilateral institutions.

20. Development Research Centre on Migration, Globalisation and Poverty (2004). Migration and pro-poor policies in Africa. A Report co-ordinated by Richard Black, Final Report.

21. Global Commission on International Migration (2005) Migration in an Interconnected World: New Directions for Action. Report of the Global Commission on International Migration. Switzerland. www.gcim.org.

22. Global Economic Prospects (2006) International Remittances and Migration. Washington DC: World Bank.

23. Government of Lesotho (2005) Kingdom of Lesotho Poverty Reduction Strategy 2004/05 - 2006/07.

Chapter 6
Investing in people

1. Population Division of the Department of Economic and Social Affairs of the United Nations Secretariat, 'World Population Prospects: The 2004 revision' www.esa.un.org/unpp

2. In sub-Saharan Africa adult literacy has risen from 28% in 1970, to 60% today, and in South and West Asia it has risen from 32% to 59%. UNESCO (2006) Education for All Global Monitoring Report. Paris: UNESCO.

3. Department for International Development, Africa Policy Department (2005) Review of Health and Education Progress in Selected African Countries. Unpublished report.

4. UNESCO (2006) Global Monitoring Report. Paris: UNESCO.

5. UN Millennium Project (2005) Investing in Development: A Practical Plan to Achieve the Millennium Development Goals. New York: United Nations. And The Commission for Africa (2005) Our Common Interest – An Argument. London: Penguin.

6. World Bank (2006) Implementing Free Primary Education. Washington DC: World Bank.

7. World Bank (2006) Global Monitoring Report, Strengthening Mutual Accountability – Aid, Trade and Governance. Washington DC: World Bank.

8. World Bank (2004) World Development Report: Making Services Work for Poor People. New York: Oxford University Press. And The Commission for Africa (2005) Our Common Interest. London: Commission for Africa. And The World Bank (2005) Global Monitoring Report. The Millennium Development Goals: From Consensus to Momentum. Washington DC: World Bank.

9. World Health Organisation (2001) Macroeconomics and Health: Investing in Health for Economic Development. Report of the Commission on Macroeconomics and Health. Geneva: WHO.

10. UNAIDS (2005) Resource needs for an expanded response to AIDS in low and middle income countries. Geneva: UNAIDS.

11. Buchan, J. and Dovlo, D. (2004) International recruitment of health workers to the UK. A Report for DFID. Unpublished. UK: DFID.

12. World Health Organisation (2006) Working Together for Health: The World Health Report 2006. Geneva: WHO.

13. James, C and others (2005) Impact on child mortality of removing user fees: simulation model. British Medical Journal. October.

14. Global Forum for Health Research (2004) Monitoring final flows for health research. Geneva: Global Forum for Health Research.

15. Environmental Resources Management (2005) Meeting the Water and Sanitation Millennium Development Goal. Unpublished report. UK: ERM.

16. Department for International Development (2005) Social transfers and chronic poverty: emerging evidence and the challenge ahead. A DFID Practice Paper. UK: DFID.

17. Karuna, P. and others (2005) Can low income countries afford basic social protection? First results of a modelling exercise. International Labour Organisation Discussion Paper 13. Geneva: ILO. And DFID (2005) Can low-income countries in Africa afford social transfers? DFID Social Protection Briefing Note No 2. November. UK: DFID.

Chapter 7
Managing climate change

1. The Inter governmental Panel on Climate Change (IPCC) was set up by the World Meteorological Organisation and the United Nations Environment Programme. It is open to all countries who are members of the UN or World Meteorological Organisation. The Secretariat, composed of climate change experts, has prepared three assessment reports about the impact of climate change, endorsed by IPCC members, of which the most recent was published in 2001. The Fourth Assessment Report is due in 2007.

2. As well as carbon dioxide, these include methane and nitrous oxide gases.

3. IPCC (2001) Summary for Policymakers: A Report of Working Group 1 of the Intergovernmental Panel on Climate Change. www.ipcc.ch/pub/spm22-01pdf

4. McCarthy and others (2001) Climate Change 2001: Impacts, Adaptation and Vulnerability. Contribution of Working Group II to the Third Assessment Report of the Inter-Governmental Panel on Climate Change. Cambridge University Press.

5. World Bank (2005) Where is the Wealth of Nations? Measuring Capital for the 21st Century. Washington DC: World Bank.

6. The UN Millennium Ecosystem Assessment estimates that 60% of environmental services are degraded or being used unsustainably and that climate change is the single most important factor that will affect environmental change over the next 50 years. Millennium Assessment (2005) Living beyond our Means. Statement of the Board of the Millennium Assessment: www.millenniumassessment.org

7. McCarthy and others (2001) Climate Change 2001: Impacts, Adaptation and Vulnerability. Contribution of Working Group II to the Third Assessment Report of the Inter-Governmental Panel on Climate Change. Cambridge University Press.

8. International Livestock Research Institute, the Energy & Resources Institute, India, and the African Centre for Technology Studies, Kenya (2006) Mapping climate vulnerability and poverty in Africa. Report to DFID.

9. OECD (2005) Bridge Over Troubled Waters: Linking Climate Change and Development. Paris: OECD.

10. Martens and others (1999) 'Climate change and future populations at risk from malaria.' Global Environmental Change: Volume 9: Supplement 1.

11. Pascual and others (2000) 'Cholera Dynamics and El Nino-Southern Oscillation.' Science. Volume 289.

12. United Nations (2001) Natural Disasters and Sustainable Development: Understanding the Links between Development, Environment and Natural Disasters, Background Paper No. 5. Secretariat for the United Nations International Strategy for Disaster Reduction: www.johannesburgsummit.org/html/documents/backgrounddocs/unisdr%20report.pdf

13. Mozambique National Disaster Management Institute.

14. Climate Analysis Indicators Tool Version 3.0 2006. This predicts that the 37 richest countries will emit 18,258 Million tonnes of carbon dioxide compared with 20,533 Million tonnes of carbon dioxide from developing countries who did not agree targets at Kyoto.

15. World Bank (2006) 'Clean Energy and Development – Towards an Investment Framework.' Paper for the Development Committee, April 2006.

16. World Bank (2006) 'Clean Energy and Development – Towards an Investment Framework' Paper for the Development Committee, April 2006.

17. The Stern Review of the Economics of Climate Change is due to report in Autumn 2006 with analysis on the economics of moving to a low carbon economy, drawing implications for timescales for action and different policies and institutions. It will also assess different approaches for adapting to climate change.

18. At Gleneagles, the G8 invited the World Bank and other multilateral development banks to develop a clean energy investment framework, to increase the volume of investments on renewable energy and energy efficiency, to identify less intensive greenhouse gas growth options and to develop local commercial capacity to develop and finance cost-effective projects that promote energy efficiency and low-carbon energy sources. See Gleneagles Plan of Action: Climate change, clean energy and sustainable development, July 2005.

19. The Clean Development Mechanism estimates there will be 950 million Carbon Emission Reduction credits (CERs) by the end of 2012 (see www.cdm.unfccc.int). On average, CERs were traded at an average of US$7 and US$11 in 2005 and 2006 respectively. Therefore, the value of the 950 million CERs will range from US$6.7 billion to US$10.5 billion. (World Bank and International Emissions Trading Association (2006) 'State and Trends of the Carbon Market 2006.' Washington DC: World Bank).

20. One proposal under consideration is a scheme that would give developing countries credit for not cutting down their forests.

21. World Bank (2006) 'Clean Energy and Development – Towards an Investment Framework' Paper for the Development Committee, April 2006.

22. Supported by DFID and the Canadian International Development Research Centre.

23. OECD DAC International Development Statistics on-line.

24. This was agreed and signed up to by UN Member States at the World Conference for Disaster Reduction, following the tsunami in 2004.

25. Our policy is explained in more detail in Department for International Development (2006) 'Reducing the Risk of Disasters – Helping to Achieve Sustainable Poverty Reduction in a Vulnerable World', DFID: London.

26. Cabot, C. and Venton, P. (2004) 'Disaster preparedness programmes in India: a cost benefit analysis' Network Paper No. 49. London: Tearfund and Overseas Development Institute. From 'Eliminating World Poverty: People and Planet' An Evidence based Analysis for the Department for International Development White Paper Consultation Process prepared by the Development and Environment Group of British and Overseas NGOs for Development.

Chapter 8
Reforming the international development system

1. This includes around 35% to the main multilateral institutions (EC, World Bank, UN and regional banks) and contributions to the main global funds such as the Global Fund to fight AIDS, TB and Malaria, the Global Alliance for Vaccines and Immunisations and the Global Environment Facility. Department for International Development (2006) Departmental Report. DFID. And, Department for International Development (2005) Statistics on International Development 2000/01 – 2004/05. DFID.

2. This chart shows UK bilateral aid as a share (7%) of total aid received by developing countries. The UK's share of total ODA in 2004, including contributions to multilateral agencies was 10%. UN includes: UNDP, UNTA, UNICEF, UNRWA, UNHCR, WFP, UNFPA and others. OECD DAC include only UN expenditure financed from un-earmarked support as multilateral. UN spending is around US$10 billion if earmarked contributions are included (UNDP figures, excluding UNHCR).

3. The nine clusters are: logistics, telecommunications, camp management, emergency shelter, health, nutrition and feeding, water and sanitation, early recovery, and protection.

4. OECD International Development Statistics (IDS) online databases on aid and other resource flows www.oecd.org/dataoecd/50/17/5037721.htm

5. The World Bank (2005) Global Monitoring Report. The Millennium Development Goals: From Consensus to Momentum. Washington DC: World Bank.

6. International Monetary Fund (2006) The Managing Director's Report on Implementing the Fund's Medium-Term Strategy. Washington DC: IMF.

7. The Commission for Africa (2005) Our Common Interest: Report of the Commission for Africa.

8. EC (2005) Highlights, Annual Report 2005 on the European Community's development policy and the implementation of external assistance in 2004. Brussels: EuropeAid Co-operation Office.

9. Ten new countries joined the EU in 2004, two are expected to become members in 2007 bringing the total to 27, and six more countries aspire to join.

10. April 2005 Commission Communication and May 2005 Council Conclusions identified 12 areas for action (trade, climate change, environment, security, agriculture, fisheries, social dimension of globalisation, migration, research and innovation, information society, transport, energy) and tasked the Commission to produce a biennial report on EU Policy Coherence for Development. May 2005 Council Conclusions asked Council to assess existing internal procedures, mechanisms and instruments to strengthen the effective integration of development concerns in its decision-making procedures on non-development policies. Also called on EU MS and Commission to strengthen policy coherence for development.

11. OECD Journal on Development, Development Co-operation Report (2005). Efforts and Policies of the Members of the Development Assistance Committee. Volume 7, Issue 1. Paris: OECD Publishing.

12. The 2005 EU Consensus on Development (SEC (2005) 929) states that "EU development policy concerns all developing countries benefiting from public development aid as listed by the OECD development aid committee" and that "the overriding objective of poverty reduction is based on the complementary aims of promoting good governance and respect for human rights, which form an integral part of long term development".

13. EC or Community aid refers to aid administered on behalf of EU Member States by the European Commission.

14. EDF is managed by the European Commission but is outside its main budget.

15. The EC plans to introduce three new geographical instruments: for countries trying to join the EU (accession countries); countries in Europe's geographical neighbourhood; and developing countries. In addition, there will be a new instrument for maintaining stability where this is threatened, alongside instruments for the other major cross-cutting issues of humanitarian aid and macro-economic support.

16. In Tanzania, an Independent Monitoring Group of advisers was set up in 2000 to mediate the aid relationship and monitor progress against specific commitments. In Mozambique, a Programme Aid Partners Performance Framework established in 2003 monitors and ranks donor performance.

17. Aid that is freely available to buy goods and services from all countries is known as 'untied aid'. Aid that is restricted to the procurement of goods and services from the donor country is known as 'tied aid.' www.webdomino1.oecd.org/comnet/dcd/untiedpubliccws.nsf

18. This graph shows aid distribution in some of the countries where DFID works. It shows that a country that is poor and performs better, can receive less aid per capita than other countries. The policy and performance ratings reflect Country Policy and Institutional Assessment (CPIA) scores, which are annual World Bank ratings. The 20% of countries with the highest CPIA scores are in the first quintile. This is a widely used measure of the likely effectiveness of aid in a country, but does not take account of other factors influencing aid effectiveness, such as post-conflict reconstruction.

19. Government of Ghana, Ministry of Education. Education Strategic Plan 2003 to 2015. Volume 1. Policies, Targets and Strategies.

Chapter 9
What can you do?

1. Excerpt from Wroe, M. and Doney, M. The rough guide to a better world and how you can make a difference. London: Rough Guides Ltd.

2. Resources produced for schools by DFID and the Department for Education and Skills for linking subjects to international development.

With thanks… This White Paper was written and produced by Catherine Masterman, Jas Malhi, Jonathan Hargreaves, Kathryn Casson, Michael Howells, Moazzam Malik (Team Leader), Richard Montgomery, Sarah MacGregor, Sarah Saxton, Tony Burdon and Veema Shah, with contributions from colleagues across DFID and other UK Government Departments and over 600 submissions during the public consultation that ran from January to April 2006.

Printed in the UK for The Stationery Office Limited on behalf of the Controller of Her Majesty's Stationery Office 7/06,5387994